THE WINNER'S CIRCLE

THE WINNER'S

Wall Street's
Best
Mutual Fund
Managers

CIRCLE

R.J. SHOOK

WILEY

John Wiley & Sons, Inc.

Published by John Wiley & Sons, Inc., Hoboken, New Jersey.
Published simultaneously in Canada.

For general information on our other products and services, or technical support, please contact our Customer Care Department within the United States at 800-762-2974, outside the United States at 317-572-3993 or fax 317-572-4002.

Designations used by companies to distinguish their products are often claimed by trademarks. In all instances where the author or publisher is aware of a claim, the product names appear in Initial Capital letters. Readers, however, should contact the appropriate companies for more complete information regarding trademarks and registration.

Wiley also publishes its books in a variety of electronic formats. Some content that appears in print may not be available in electronic books.

For more information about Wiley products, visit our web site at www.wiley.com.

Library of Congress Cataloging-in-Publication Data:

Shook, R. J. (Robert James)
    The winner's circle : Wall Street's best mutual fund managers / R.J. Shook.
      p. cm.
    Includes index.
    ISBN 0-471-67914-3 (cloth)
  1. Mutual funds—United States. 2. Investment advisors—United States. 3. Success in business. I. Title.
  HG4930.S464 2005
  332.63'27'092273—dc22

2004009875

Printed in the United States of America.

10 9 8 7 6 5 4 3 2 1

To my grandparents, Belle and Herb . . . with all my love.

CONTENTS

ACKNOWLEDGMENTS

I would like to express how honored I am that Don Phillips wrote my Foreword. As Morningstar managing director, Don is one of the most influential individuals in the industry; both Wall Street and investors around the globe have benefited from his leadership and innovations.

Special gratitude is due to the mutual fund managers profiled in *The Winner's Circle*, all of whom I have come to admire and respect. I deeply value the friendships that have developed along the way. These portfolio managers need not seek publicity, for their immense success keeps them busy managing hundreds of billions of dollars for millions of investors worldwide. In virtually all cases, their motives for participating were altruistic and magnanimous. In most cases, the managers expressed to me their greatest satisfaction: helping investors reach their needs, objectives, and dreams. John Calamos of Calamos Funds told me one of his favorite days: "The day a gentleman walked into our office to personally thank us for helping him comfortably reach his retirement." John walked him around the office to meet the team.

A special thank-you to my publisher, John Wiley & Sons—in particular: executive editor Debra Englander for her deep expertise and talent, and her team, including Michael Lisk and Greg Friedman.

Of course, my team is due much credit. Little would be accomplished without immense support from Debra Thompson and Eric Johnston, as well as editorial support from Rebecca McReynolds, Dom Delprete, and Ellen Uzelac.

I am thankful for the brilliance of Al Zuckerman, one of the publishing world's greatest, for his ideas, insights, and endless wisdom.

FOREWORD

*L*earning insights from Wall Street's best portfolio managers is incredibly smart for any investor, and R.J. Shook provides an excellent conduit through *The Winner's Circle*. It makes perfect sense to see what the great investors have done. In every other field of endeavor, from the arts to medicine to sports, people turn to the best practitioners to learn how they succeeded.

The irony is that when it comes to investments, university classes teach the theory of investing—that markets are efficient and you can't beat them. This is the equivalent of saying that there are rules of literature, and if you don't follow them, you can't write a great novel. The managers profiled in this book have long-term track records—many of them through multiple bear and bull markets—that have stood the test of time.

R.J. Shook is essentially providing readers a unique opportunity to spend a day with 14 outstanding portfolio managers and learn how they think and how they process information to make their investment decisions. Discovering how these managers invest, the mistakes they have made and since learned from, how they think, and what they have studied over time is extremely relevant to individual investors.

Of course, individual investors have more freedom than the typical money manager. The professionals have to worry about their quarterly performances, whether their track record will fall off and hurt their rankings, and so on. But individuals can emulate these professional money managers—even by picking and choosing investing styles and ideas—and Shook has selected the crème de la crème from which to choose.

In *The Winner's Circle* readers get an inside—and rare—view on what makes these managers tick and why their particular investment style works. By looking at the market through their eyes, individuals can begin to develop their own approach to the markets.

The best money managers—those in this book—have the courage to be different from the crowd. They are not afraid to be out of step with the rest of the market. They manage risk. They think differently. And their disciplines remain steadfast. These are the best role models for individual investors.

In this book, we learn that investing doesn't have to be complicated. A commonsense approach—with a long-term horizon and discipline—is usually a sound strategy for most investors.

R.J. Shook has chosen a diverse group of people from John Calamos of Calamos Growth Fund and Wallace Weitz of Weitz Partners Value Fund to Richie Freeman of the Smith Barney Aggressive Growth Fund and Bill Miller of the Legg Mason Value Trust. Their approaches are unique, and this is an important lesson for readers. Individuals must determine which philosophy and which approach are right for their "investing personality." This book provides an excellent way for investors to begin to discern their investing personality. And by picking managers based on long-term risk-adjusted parameters, as well as a qualitative approach, Shook provides a smart blueprint toward building a well-diversified portfolio of mutual funds.

—Don Phillips
Managing Director, Morningstar, Inc.

INTRODUCTION

Don't be fooled. These outstanding mutual fund managers make investing look easy—the same way we may watch a professional athlete make a great play or a great actor perform. With these mutual fund managers sharing their secrets, you may be tempted to do it yourself. I strongly encourage you to invest *with* them, not *like* them.

I have a confession: Prior to interviewing these mutual fund managers, I was devoted to managing my own stock and bond portfolios. After all, I was a financial advisor and an analyst on Wall Street for over a decade. Why pay unnecessary and ongoing fees when I can buy stocks and bonds with a onetime—and often negligible—commission. When appropriate, I would rebalance based on my feeling of where there markets were headed. I could control my own destiny. I was satisfied with my performance, even through the down markets in the early 2000s.

That is no longer true. After interviewing these mutual fund managers, also referred to as portfolio managers, I realized that competing against them in the long term is the equivalent of taking on basketball-great Michael Jordan in a game of one-on-one—it's no contest, especially when you calculate the added risk we usually incur for an improperly structured portfolio. Individual investors—even well over 99 percent of all portfolio managers—aren't even in the same league as these *Winner's Circle* managers. Not only can I not invest like them (on a short-term basis, anyone can get lucky, but in the long-term it is not even a competition), I cannot even think like them (more on this later). The only way I will ever invest is through a professional portfolio manager, like the ones profiled in this book (through a financial advisor, I have placed my money in each of their funds). And to ensure diversified holdings and a disciplined asset allocation strategy, I choose to trust a professional financial advisor, someone with the highest levels of integrity, professionalism, and skills—someone who embodies the characteristics of a *Winner's Circle* financial advisor (another line of books in which I specialize). The powerful combination of all-star portfolio managers with a trusted financial advisor who is helping me obtain my goals, objectives, and dreams enables me to effectively compete as if I have a whole team of Michael Jordans working for me.

While there is a lot of publicity surrounding high expenses associated with "loaded" funds (as opposed to no-load funds, which maintain smaller expense ratios in order to deliver higher returns), I take George Steinbrenner's approach: Pay up for proven talent. After all, George's Yankees deliver enormous revenue streams due to their ability to bankroll an unprecedented level of talent compared to most other ballclubs. They win games, period. For a little added expense, would you bet on an entire team of Michael Jordans or settle for the benchwarmers? (Richard Aster's Meridian Value Fund, Wallace Weitz's Weitz Partners Value Fund and Bob Rodriguez's FPA New Income, Inc. are no-load funds.)

I have become expert in evaluating financial advisors, and have interviewed hundreds of the best in the industry. Qualitatively, I know who the best financial advisors in the business are. I leverage this capability to evaluate similar qualities in mutual fund managers.

Unwavering Integrity and Principles—A Qualitative Approach

The mutual fund managers profiled in this book are truly champions. Yes, they have provided outstanding returns for their shareholders, all consistently beating their benchmark indexes and competing funds in their categories over the long term on a risk-adjusted basis. Perhaps what impresses me most is their dedication to their investors. After spending hours interviewing each of these champions, it became abundantly clear that they truly care about their investors. While they may be managing tens of billions of dollars, they really care about each individual behind each dollar that is entrusted to them. In many cases they describe their greatest satisfaction as occurring when they receive a letter or handshake with the words: "Thanks to you, I was able to send my children to college." Because of this high regard for their investors, it came as no surprise that these managers were not implicated in the scandals. Greed is the furthest thing from these managers' minds.

Characteristics of Wall Street's Best Mutual Fund Managers

Foremost, these portfolio managers are passionate about investing; they love their careers and the teams they have created. They are humble, and seek to give much credit to their teams (some managers, like Oppenheimer's Bill Wilby and AXA Rosenberg's Bill Ricks, both insisted that they are successful because of their team, and if given a choice would prefer to have their entire team in the spotlight, and not themselves solely). They are all quick to admit mistakes they have made, but feel the experience has only made them better. As Wall Street's best, they do have egos, but not the self-serving kind. Their egos are driven by the success of their shareholders.

Unlike most portfolio managers, the *Winner's Circle* mutual fund managers stick to their disciplines, and never stray. Franklin Templeton's Jeff Everett, a disciple of legendary investor Sir John Templeton, maintains Sir John's disciplines, and when new circumstances arise does not hesitate to talk through situations with his mentor. Using hundreds of metrics, AXA Rosenberg's quantitative models follow strict instructions, never deviating from Bill Ricks and team's investment approach.

These managers are students of the world, and masters of investing. Davis Funds' Chris Davis could be the CEO of many large corporations; Legg Mason's Bill Miller might be one of the deepest thinkers I have ever met. Eaton Vance's subadvisor Sam Isaly and his team, with their doctors, Ph.D.s and MBAs, could build a formidable biotechnology company.

While these managers consider themselves lifelong students of the markets, they are indeed the leading experts in their fields, and forging new frontiers. Calamos Funds' John Calamos, author of *Convertible Securities: The Latest Instruments, Portfolio Strategies, and Valuation Analysis* (McGraw-Hill Trade, 2nd edition, June 1, 1998) is considered the leading authority of convertible-bond investing, an approach he uses when investing in mid-cap growth stocks. David Dreman practically invented the concept of contrarian investing, and documented groundbreaking ideas in many of his books, including his first: *Psychology and the Stock Market: Investment Strategy Beyond Random Walk* (Amacom, 1977).

Interestingly, each manager thinks independently. They are never coerced by current sentiments or newspaper headlines. They are trained to think differently; for most of them, when the crowds are heading in one direction, they are going the other way. I recall a conversation with David Dreman in mid-2002 where he seemed excited at the opportunity to buy Tyco in the low teens, after falling from around $60 a share. While the newspapers and market commentators were predicting the company would go belly-up, this manager was buying as much as his disciplines would permit. By 2004 he had more than doubled his money. He told me: "We believe the panic over accounting practices is overdone, and Tyco will survive." These managers patiently wait for the right time to buy or sell a stock or bond; once it hits their thoroughly analyzed targets, they buy with conviction of their analyses, not with emotions. Their holding periods, for the most part, are far longer than the peers in their mutual fund categories.

I find it interesting that while the above-mentioned traits and characteristics may seem intuitive or commonsense, they are just not shared by most portfolio managers.

Selection Criteria

To qualify as a *Winner's Circle* mutual fund manager, each individual is subjected to intense scrutiny, based on several weighted criteria. The process begins by seeking lead managers, whether they are the sole managers or part of a team. The first criterion in determining the top fund managers is tenure—a portfolio manager must have been at the helm of his or her fund for a minimum of five years; each manager must have at least a 10-year performance record in which *The Winner's Circle* evaluates performance. Managers in each category are evaluated against peers (throughout the book, *peers or peer groups* refer to the described fund's category of other similar funds, such as large-cap value or small-cap growth; unless otherwise noted, peers usually refers to fund-tracking firm Morningstar, Inc.'s analysis); compound rates of return are assessed primarily over a 10-year period, and lesser weightings for three- and five-year periods. Greater weightings are given to managers with lengthier tenures, such as David Dreman's several-decades'-worth of extraordinary measured performance.

When measuring a manager's performance in comparison to his or her peer group in terms of performance, *The Winner's Circle* diligently examines risk; clearly, looking only at a portfolio's returns ignores risk, the other important half of an investment equation. A manager that consistently beats the competition may also be one that is taking on more risk. Therefore, risk-adjusted returns are the basis of performance measures. Other factors include: stability of management, risk sensitivity, up-market and down-market performance, tax minimization, expenses, and predictability of returns.

The Winner's Circle examines the best mutual fund managers in each of the following categories:

Stock Funds Winners

1. Large-Cap Growth   Richie Freeman, Smith Barney
        Aggressive Growth

2. Large-Cap Value   David Dreman, Scudder-Dreman
        High Return Equity Fund

3. Large-Cap Core   William H. Miller III, Legg Mason
        Value Trust

4. Large-Cap Relative Value   Christopher C. Davis, Davis New York
        Venture Fund

5. Mid-Cap Growth   John Calamos, Calamos Growth Fund

6. Mid–Cap Value   Wallace R. Weitz, Weitz Partners Value Fund
7. Mid–Cap Core   Richard F. Aster, Jr., Meridian Value Fund
8. Small–Cap Growth   Jeff Cardon, Wasatch Small Cap
                             Growth Fund
9. Small–Cap Value   Joel C. Tillinghast, Fidelity Low-Priced
                             Stock Fund
10. Small–Cap Core   Bill Ricks and Team, AXA Rosenberg
                             U.S. Small Cap
11. World Equities   Bill Wilby, Oppenheimer Global Fund
12. Foreign Value   Jeff Everett, Templeton Foreign Fund

Sector Fund Winner

13. Health/Biotechnology   Sam Isaly, Eaton Vance Worldwide Health
                             Sciences Fund

Bond Fund Winner

14. Intermediate-Term   Bob Rodriguez, FPA New Income, Inc.
    Investment Grade

I always emphasize the value of diversification. It is my belief that these *Winner's Circle* mutual fund managers are an excellent starting point when building a diversified portfolio.

You'll notice that I detail the backgrounds of these portfolio managers, and even include mistakes and blunders these champions have encountered. This is an excellent way to learn about their characters, values, and principles. I would recommend all of these funds as part of a well-diversified portfolio for my grandmother (I own these funds, as do my young children).

You'll also learn how these champions defined their niche, and became better than any other investor in that category. Join me as we delve into how they developed their investing strategies, disciplines, and philosophies. You will pick up many investing strategies and learn how opportunities are discovered. In the end, you'll learn money-management secrets typically reserved for elite investors.

PART I

, , ,

Large–Cap
Mutual Fund Managers

CHAPTER ONE

RICHIE FREEMAN

SMITH BARNEY
AGGRESSIVE
GROWTH FUND

❜❜❜

To Richie Freeman, the fund he manages, Smith Barney Aggressive Growth Fund, is more than just a collection of $8.0 billion in investor assets; it is a collection of individuals who entrust him with their college money, savings for a new home, a comfortable retirement, and other dreams. Managing individuals' money is not just a career for Richie; it has been his lifetime passion. While his track record speaks for itself—during the 10-year period through 2003 the fund returned a compound, annualized 15.04 percent to his investors, nearly four percentage points better than the S&P 500 and almost six percentage points better than the Morningstar average peer fund in the large-cap growth category (Morningstar currently ranks his performance as number one over this time horizon)—he is simply determined to make money for his investors.

Indeed, his winning performance is based on a philosophy that he began developing at 13 years of age. Up until that point, the youngster had only aspired to be a baseball player. Little did he know that he would be given a present that would forever change his life.

Richie's father, Ted, deserves the credit for having nurtured his interest in the stock market. In the early 1960s, Ted placed some of Richie's savings into a mutual fund, helping drive home the benefits of diversification to the young investor. In an oft-repeated expression, Ted would tell young Rich, "One day you will work hard for your money. You should always remember to make your money work hard for you." While some relatives thought it wrong to allow a youngster to spend time hanging around a brokerage office, Ted and Richie's mother Eleonor encouraged Richie. "Sitting in that brokerage office on Kings Highway in Brooklyn was the best undergraduate training a stock market enthusiast could get," says Richie today.

In 1966, for his Bar Mitzvah, Richie received as gifts shares in several companies, including AJ Industries, an industrial concern. Routinely, Richie would wait for the late edition of the *New York Post* to check the closing prices on his stocks. Ted would regularly explain to him why the value of his positions, and thus his savings, fluctuated in price that day. Astonished that investors would change their minds so frequently about the value of his stocks, Richie sought more current information. Every day the market was open, after school and a game of stickball in Brooklyn, Richie would walk to the local brokerage office to check the tape.

In fact, during the mid-sixties, the teenager spent almost as much time watching the local stockbroker's ticker tape as he did playing stickball in the schoolyards of Brooklyn. The financial pages of his father's *New York Post* continued to fascinate him. In addition to looking at closing stock prices, he liked to tally up his mutual funds' stock positions to see how they performed for the day.

While other investors watching the ticker tape were calculating the gains and losses of their positions, Richie was doing something different. He was visualizing trends in stock prices, noticing distinct patterns in the way the stocks traded, realizing the forces behind supply and demand. Even now he says, "I don't think there's a better way to learn about the market than being intimately involved while watching the tape, really living and breathing it. At first glance the flashing numbers might appear as tedium or monotony, but after a while you will notice certain price trends developing." So enchanted was young Richie by his study of the ticker tape that, as he now admits, he "hated weekends because the markets were closed."

Every day after the market closed, Richie would estimate the value of his mutual fund holdings. Using an old Burroughs adding machine, he calculated the overall value of his mutual funds by totaling up the value of the individual holdings in the funds. The next day, he would see how close his calculation came to the published value of the fund. By the time he was 15, with his parents' permission, he was investing with his own stockbroker. "This is where I really earned my business degree," he says. "There was no better training than studying the ticker tape and investing for myself." Richie still maintains contact with his childhood stockbroker. Coincidentally, Richie and the broker now both work for Citigroup, although in different divisions.

He gives a short laugh, and describes summertime visits to another broker's office back in the sixties. "As a camp counselor in Port Jervis, New York, I would treat the kids to a hike into town so I could spend time in the brokerage office watching the ticker tape. I convinced them that the exercise was good for them."

Richie graduated from Brooklyn College and received an MBA in finance from New York University. In 1983, after spending eight years as a research analyst on Wall Street, Richie was asked to help launch a new fund, then known as the Shearson Aggressive Growth Fund. He still manages that very same fund, which is now known as the Smith Barney Aggressive Growth Fund. (Smith Barney Asset Management is part of Citigroup Asset Management.)

Though Richie tends to take less risk than his average peer, the fund has been marketed as an aggressive fund, mostly due to its exposure to small- and mid-cap stocks. Because of Richie's conservative nature, he encourages investors to diversify by maintaining only a portion of their portfolio in the fund. Even so, Richie treats the money as if it is 100 percent of everyone's money. "This isn't a game, and this isn't play money," he maintains. "I take this to heart—I hate to lose."

Richie likes to use baseball metaphors when discussing the markets, comparing the way he composes his stock portfolio to creating a baseball team. "Like a good baseball manager, my job is to evaluate individual talent and build the players into a cohesive team. Similarly, I focus on picking great individual companies that can collectively result in great performance for the fund over the long haul." During the rare times he takes away from the markets, he will check Yankees and Mets scores and statistics. His office is adorned with pictures of his family and baseball memorabilia.

The Smith Barney Aggressive Growth Fund was established to seek capital appreciation among companies that meet Richie's valuation metrics: stocks he believes will surpass the S&P 500 Index's average earnings growth. Richie has always believed that the largest gains can be earned by identifying great growth companies early in their life cycles, when they are relatively undiscovered small- or mid-cap stocks, and then holding them for the long-term. As long as the fundamental reasons he invested in a company remain intact, and revenues and earnings continue to grow, Richie tends to hold the position, sometimes even after it becomes a large-cap company.

Richie began to really feel the pressure of investing other people's money his first full calendar year on the job. It was 1984: The fund was down 12.2 percent for the year. While he harbored doubts about his ability, Richie nevertheless had the confidence in his companies to hold on and let them grow.

"I used to go home complaining to my wife Randi, 'Boy, did I make a mistake,' " he remembers. "And to add to my enormous sense of responsibility and my keen awareness of the trust that investors were placing in me, my performance was posted in the paper every day! This obsession has never gone away. If anything, it has probably increased."

One of the mid-cap companies he was buying in 1984 was a microchip manufacturer, little known at the time, called Intel. The purchase was considered a brash move at the time as the investing world believed Japan was going to dominate the computer chip market into the future. Richie saw another story; he saw a company whose stock was trading at a split-adjusted average price of 88 cents, with unique products and a management team with a solid track record. He also believed that the company was intelligent enough to invest massive sums of money in research and development to create the next generation of chips. Richie believed in the company's philosophy and positioning of its products. Now, nearly 20 years later, the chipmaker's market cap exceeds $200 billion. Richie likens this pick to the Mets picking catcher Mike Piazza, who is considered the best offensive catcher in the history of baseball. "The Mets picking Piazza is like me picking Intel a couple decades ago," Richie says, modestly attributing the pick to good luck. Other portfolio holdings that were purchased at the beginning of the fund's life and remain in the fund today include Forest Labs and Comcast.

Because of his buy-and-hold approach, Richie has earned a reputation on the Street as a "patient" investor. Richie believes that a true growth portfolio should consist of companies that can be held not for a quarter or two, but for many years so that the earnings growth can compound over time.

When selecting stocks, Richie uses a bottom-up approach, a technique that focuses on individual company fundamentals to find attractive opportunities, as opposed to a top-down method that focuses on broad economic and industry trends to identify interesting stocks. He considers himself a stock picker, not a market forecaster, opting for companies that can, in some cases, control their own destinies.

Using this approach, Richie seeks stocks that he anticipates may appreciate over a three- to five-year time frame. Unlike many aggressive growth investors, who employ a momentum strategy in buying stocks that are widely held and rapidly rising in price, Richie likes to explore areas that Wall Street has not yet discovered. He will seek out small, relatively unknown companies well before they have hit Wall Street's radar screen; generally they are not even covered by Street analysts. This strategy can give Richie's fund a tremendous boost as these stocks continue to exhibit strong growth, drawing the attention of Wall Street and the brokerage networks. Once recognized by Wall Street and the investing public, the prices of these stocks can appreciate significantly.

Overall, when looking for companies that are likely to become long-term winners, Richie forgoes rigid stock screening tools when narrowing down his potential targets. First, he looks at the management team, scrutinizing their experience and track records, and determining how those experiences would help in the new venture. He is a big believer in direct contact with management, spending time talking to management and interviewing them to better understand their skills, their philosophies, and their intentions for leading the company into the future.

Furthermore, Richie prefers that a significant portion of management compensation be tied to the performance of the company stock, thereby aligning management's interests with those of the shareholder. As he often quips, "If a stock performs poorly on any given day, I want management to go home feeling just as bad as I do."

To illustrate, in 1992 Richie bought shares in Infinity Broadcasting when it went public. He was particularly interested in the company's predictable and growing cash flow, and in CEO Mel Karmazin's exceptional capabilities in managing profitable broadcasting properties. Richie was also alert to the CEO's personal stake in the company, which was most of his Karmazin's net worth. Westinghouse acquired Infinity in 1996. Later, Westinghouse divested its industrial operations and changed its name to CBS in order to focus on its media operations. CBS merged with Viacom in 2001 and Karmazin remained with the combined company as president and COO until his departure in 2004. "Mel Karmazin is a good example of the type of manager I look for. He has an exceptional track record and his interests are aligned with shareholders." With Viacom trading in the mid-30s, Richie's adjusted cost basis is just over $2 per share.

While Richie considers management a key component in narrowing down his stock selection, he believes that even the best management team cannot effectively execute without the right goods or services. He looks for companies that have products or services that customers are virtually compelled to use, such as medicines that effectively treat serious diseases. "We invest in long-term trends, not fads," he says.

Richie wants to feel comfortable knowing that earnings and cash flow are likely to be healthy going out at least three years. He will generally consider an investment in a not-yet-profitable company if it has the potential to become profitable within a two- to three-year period, and has the cash to support the business in the meantime. The company must also have a solid balance sheet with little or no debt. However, some industries that have predictable cash flows may use debt as a financing vehicle. Then he compares the stock's current valuation with the projected earnings growth rate he forecasts for the company. He is less interested in companies that are trading at valuation levels more than two times their annualized earnings growth rate. The price-earnings-to-growth (PEG) ratio helps to determine a stock's value while taking into account earnings growth; it is particularly helpful when valuing companies that pay no dividends, such as small- and mid-cap growth stocks. "We want growth companies, but we want to buy them on the cheap," he says.

Here Richie offers an example. About a decade ago, he initiated a small position in Idec Pharmaceuticals. Subsequently, the biopharmaceutical company's leading product, Rituxan, a drug therapy for treating non-Hodgkin's lymphoma, proved effective in clinical trials, giving Richie the confidence to increase his stake in Idec. He believed the drug was unquestionably the right drug, one that many doctors would prescribe for non-Hodgkin's lymphoma once it earned approval. Even though Richie believed in the product, to him Idec was still an unproven company. One advantage: Richie had confidence in the CEO, who had a successful track record at Genentech. "I like to invest with people who have great track records at successful companies—especially if I've been successful with them in the past." Richie adds: "I also call it betting on the jockeys." Here Richie started with a modest position and then added to it, buying the micro-cap stock at a split-adjusted average price of $2 per share in the mid-nineties when its market capitalization was around $50 million. Idec recently merged with Biogen to form Biogen Idec, the world's third largest biotechnology firm.

When looking at a company's fundamentals, Richie says, "First, I look to see if the company's product has longevity. Is the product unique enough that the company will be able to sustain an advantage over potential competitors? If the product is not so unique, then you want to pay a lower price for the stock to compensate for the risk that competing products will take market share."

Richie will typically put 1 to 3 percent of the fund's assets in a new stock position. "This isn't a set number because there are so many factors," he says, such as his comfort level with risk. "As I become more comfortable that the risk level is diminishing—and hopefully the stock hasn't moved up much—then I might add to the position." In many cases, a stock may drop soon after he buys it, but he remains unfazed: "Of course, any investor would like to see everyone else jump in on a stock after you buy it, but it just doesn't happen like that; I don't get upset if the idea doesn't catch on right away," he says. "As long as my conviction remains, I'm not afraid to build a position if a stock is dropping, and I'm not afraid to go against common wisdom on the Street." The Idec investment proved to be a classic Richie Freeman investment: taking a small position in an immature company, then increasing the position as the company successfully proves its ability to grow.

"When it comes to earnings," says Richie, "I try to make my best judgment over a three-year period." This approach differentiates him from the legions of others who look only at the next quarter or six months. "As a disciplined, long-term investor, I have to count on companies missing their earnings expectations to some degree. Even companies such as Intel and Forest Labs have missed numbers. I'm more interested in whether a company is capable of achieving higher highs in earnings and cash flow over time. I can tolerate short-term disappointments if the long-term results remain strong."

Another prime example of buying early is Comcast Corporation, an operator of cable networks and programming, which Richie began buying in 1983. Comcast had a solid management team. Also, the company pursued an acquisition strategy that enabled it to steadily increase its cash flow. Richie bought more stock in 1996 because he believed that cable would become the method of choice for delivering information. Shortly thereafter, Bill Gates invested $1 billion in the company, further validating Richie's belief in cable as a major player in the broadband arena.

Richie avoided the dot-com bubble because he "couldn't place a value on the companies," he says. While many money managers ignored the lack of earnings and focused on the go-go momentum of technology stocks, Richie held tight to his valuation discipline, steering clear of the sector and largely avoiding massive losses when the bubble burst in early 2000. In 1997, however, he was able to place a value on one technology company, Netscape Communications. America Online, which itself merged with Time Warner, eventually acquired the company.

In the biotechnology sector, Richie invests mainly in companies that are already profitable or, in his opinion, have the potential to become profitable within a three-year period. Richie believes one trend in the biotech sector will continue. "Large pharmaceutical companies will continue to partner with smaller companies that have promising products," he explains. "The larger company will arrange very favorable royalty structures for the drugs, and may take an equity stake in the smaller company."

Because of Richie's bottom-up approach, some industry sectors may represent heavier weightings than others in the fund. This is especially true, considering that the portfolio may contain anywhere from 60 to 80 holdings. He limits any single holding to 10 percent of the fund's assets, thus avoiding overconcentration. The biggest reason he will sell a stock is to minimize its relative size in the portfolio. Instead of selling an entire position because of its size, Richie will merely "trim it down."

Richie generally has low turnover in his portfolio, believing that if a portfolio of growth stocks is designed properly, stocks should be held for the long haul.

The turnover of stocks in Richie's portfolio is relatively small when compared with that of his peers. With a historic annualized turnover of 5 to 10 percent, the average stock is held an almost unheard-of 14 years (over the last three years, the fund's annual turnover was only 1 percent); compare this with the average large-cap growth funds' turnover rate of

138 percent, which equates to the average stock being held less than nine months. This low turnover has made Richie's fund more tax efficient than 99 percent of all his peers over the last three and five years. While growth-stock funds actively trade securities to seek the best possible performance, Richie believes it is more important to understand the companies in a portfolio and to stick to a long-term plan. Another distinguishing feature is expenses that are well below his peers' average, which is helpful when seeking the maximum total return.

Just how good are Richie's returns? To put it simply, Richie is one of the premier growth stock investors of the last 20 years. If you invested in his fund when it began on October 24, 1983 and held it through year-end 2003, you would have a 1,440.49 percent total return on your investment, an annualized equivalent return of 14.5 percent. Over the same time period (beginning November 1, 1983), the S&P 500 index advanced 1069.22 percent, while the average fund competitor was up only 724.21 percent, or 11.03 percent on an annualized basis. Richie outperformed every peer. Additionally, he is ranked in the top 1 percent of his peers over the past five and ten years. Factor in risk-adjusted returns and he looks even better.

Ranked as the best in his category, Richie is the first to admit that you can't rest on your laurels; that's the time, he says, to give up management of the fund. His measure of success is his ability to make his investors money, not simply beating an index or competitor; in fact, he likes to see other managers do well because he likes to see all investors do well. He deplores the constant, daily measuring of one manager's performance against another's. "I just want to be the best I can for my investors; I never look at success in terms of me being in the top quartile or top 1 percent."

What has changed over the couple of decades he has been managing the Smith Barney Aggressive Growth Fund? Not much: His winning investing style, developed early in his career, is placing him at the top of the large-cap growth fund managers category; he still watches the ticker tape (though now it scrolls across a computer monitor); and he follows baseball as enthusiastically as he did as a child.

But some things *do* change: He no longer hates the fact that markets are closed on the weekends, he concedes with a smile. "That's when I get to spend time with my wife and two daughters.

Getting to know Richie means understanding his true loves in life. Besides family, and the markets, he is still passionate about baseball. And while he may fret that he will never play in the majors, today he is an all-star mutual fund manager, batting far better than any other large-cap growth fund manager around, according to *Winner's Circle* research.

CHAPTER TWO

DAVID DREMAN

SCUDDER-DREMAN
HIGH RETURN
EQUITY FUND

› › ›

The *New York Times* calls him the "Grand Master." *Barron's* calls him a "Pro." On Wall Street he is known as the "King of Contrarians." *The Winner's Circle* ranks him as the best large-cap value fund manager anywhere.

With nearly three decades' worth of successful investing to his credit, David Dreman's name has become synonymous with *contrarian investing*. Over the last decade alone his Scudder-Dreman High Return Equity Fund has clobbered its benchmark S&P 500 by almost three percentage points—and his average peer by almost four percentage points—through December 2003 with a return of 13.71 percent. While countless others have tried to emulate his strategy, he remains inimitable, consistently besting competitors with his long-proven strategy.

Spending the better part of an afternoon interviewing David in his office, I was impressed beyond my highest expectations. Beside his extraordinary investing accomplishments, David has high academic qualifications, and is a well-regarded author and a regular *Forbes* magazine contributor. Soft-spoken, humorous, and charismatic, he is always willing to offer his knowledge to large or small investors. Delving into the mind of one of our era's greatest investors, I was able to uncover the ideologies and principles behind his brilliant strategy.

Background and Education

To best understand David, I found, one must go back to his early life in Winnipeg, Canada. Born in 1936 into a tightly knit family, David had a

normal Canadian childhood—lots of ice hockey, skating, and skiing—
with one exception: Beginning at age three, he spent a good portion of
his youth on the Winnipeg Commodities trading floor, the biggest of its
kind in Canada. His father, with whom he had a close relationship, traded
in the pits and regularly brought his young son to work. Some of David's
earliest memories are of the activity and buzz of the trading floor. As he
grew older, he marveled at his father's trading ability. Even though his father traded against the crowd, he was consistently very successful, considered one of the best. In fact, the Canadian Exchange established an award
in memory of his commitment to the highest level of ethics and success
in trading.

David didn't realize it at the time, of course, but he was receiving from
his father perhaps the first-ever formal training in contrarian investing. As
busy as his father was trading, he took the time to explain to young David
exactly which decisions proved right and which proved wrong. Thus, as a
teenager, David could tell you that large investors, even the brokerage
houses, tended to follow the current trends, and why that proved wrong
more often than right.

By the time he entered the University of Manitoba he considered himself a contrarian in economics and a contrarian in investment theory. "Before you can consider yourself a contrarian today, you must be formally
schooled," David says, perhaps thinking back to his decade-and-a-half of
experience in the trenches before he left home for college. "I was schooled
in the traditional way, but I always questioned the traditional methods." In
particular, he always had reservations about certain evaluation techniques
used by analysts.

The basic tenet of the contrarian philosophy is that investors are driven by irrationalities, which leads to anomalies in the market. This op-
poses the widely accepted *efficient market* theory that (1) investors act
rationally, and (2) all information is immediately factored in the prices
of stocks so that it is not possible to beat the market consistently. Behavioral finance, a philosophy related to contrarian investing, is the study of
the financial markets that integrates psychology and economics. (In

2002 the Noble Prize in Economics was awarded for the first time in this field.)

Contrarian Research Beginnings

David graduated with a major in business and an MBA in finance (he later received an honorary doctorate from the university), and promised himself one year on Wall Street in order to carefully study the markets before heading back to Manitoba. "The U.S. markets have always been far more volatile than the Canadian markets," he says, "so I felt Wall Street was the right setting to study market behavior."

Hired as an analyst by Value Line in the mid-1960s, he was given $15,000 a year to pick stocks. His hard work and ability to spot value in the marketplace won him a spot picking stocks for a growth mutual fund. While he proved successful, he felt that he had not yet mastered his contrarian philosophy, and so he left the fund to do his own research. This research led to his first book, *Psychology and the Stock Market: Investment Strategy Beyond Random Walk* (Amacom, 1977). At this point, David knew that New York—the financial capital of the world—was where he belonged.

His two-year research hiatus began after the bear markets of 1973 and 1974. As stocks became overvalued during the late sixties and into the early seventies, David wondered why Wall Street was so enthusiastic about them. Then the bear markets hit; those same stocks were 90 percent cheaper, and no one wanted to touch them. With hard assets selling at a fraction of their breakup value, David was determined to figure out why investors avoided stocks like the plague, whereas he saw only value.

"This behavioral finance fascinated me," David begins, as he discusses his groundbreaking book, one of the first to broach the subject of behavioral finance. "It was really about why people consistently make mistakes. These analysts and money managers are extremely bright individuals, but I identified some real reasons why they tend to follow the crowd. For example, why do they tend to throw away their formal training to pursue mistakes, which they later regret and agree never to do again? My first book enabled me to thoroughly explore and research these events that I was witnessing," David says, looking back to the contrarian training he had been receiving since early childhood. "I just felt that with all these warnings there had to be a better way to invest."

David was initially reluctant to publish the book, given that the facts he had discovered did not paint a pretty picture of Wall Street professionals. "I thought I might be alienated from Wall Street," he says with a short laugh. However, David's book was extremely well received. In fact, many money managers called him, praising him for his insights and asking him for advice.

In 1977, shortly after the book was published, David was asked to lead the research efforts at a Wall Street firm. Later, he was asked to manage money by institutional investors, and started his own company—a predecessor to Dreman Value Management, which now manages the Scudder-Dreman High Return Equity Fund. Since its beginning, the money management company has been based entirely on the contrarian investing principles set forth in his books. Although David had money waiting in line to be invested with him, he still felt the pains of starting a new business. "I really had to focus on building a team that could support my investing processes, and enable me to spend my time doing what I do best—managing money."

Meanwhile, he was working nights and weekends to expand the research of the first book by adding specific landmark contrarian strategies, such as investing in out-of-favor stocks, which he found outperformed their in-favor counterparts. These new discoveries were published in his 1980 book, *Contrarian Investment Strategy* (published by Dreman Contrarian Group). "My first book covered the psychological aspects of markets and the influence of psychology on investing," he says. "Regardless of their formal training in finance or their financial backgrounds, people tend to make the same psychological mistakes over and over again." *Contrarian Investment Strategy* covers many of the mistakes that most investors tend to make, while focusing on the contrarian methods that David has developed in great detail. The book was hailed as groundbreaking by the *New York Times* and major Wall Street firms.

Contrarian Strategy at Work

Contrarian Investment Strategy generated so much positive publicity that not only were the money managers calling him for advice, but investors called him, asking him to manage their money. "I never realized that my research would ever lead to money management," he says, still startled by the evolution of his career.

After five years, David had a solid track record, outperforming both the S&P 500 and his average peer. An avalanche of new money flowed into his firm. His clients consisted of both institutional and high-net-worth accounts. By 1985, value stocks had posted impressive returns versus other sectors, mainly growth stocks, for several years. Investors started believing that value had seen its day and would never come back; consequently, value stocks dropped in price, enabling David to buy more of them. A year or so later, value stocks came back, positioning David's investors with big gains.

By this time, David had made a name for himself and his firm and had fine-tuned his investment philosophy. "We're really value investors," he says. "We buy stocks when they're priced low to earnings, priced low to cash flow, priced low to book value, and we prefer to buy these stocks if they provide an attractive yield. When we buy the stocks with low price-earnings (P/E) ratios, we're most interested in them if they're under the market's average P/E ratio."

Why Follow the Crowd?

With his investment philosophy fully validated by scores of research and studies, David still wondered why Wall Street insisted on being part of the herd. "It fascinated me that Wall Street has had thousands of books published on how to make money in the markets, but there's no proof that any of them really work." All of David's books are packed full of statistics that are the basis for his principles. "My investing methodology is backed by statistics that prove, for example, that the strategy of investing in stocks with low P/E ratios works," he continues, describing one methodology that he has carefully analyzed going all the way back to 1930 in his third book, *Contrarian Investment Strategies: The Next Generation* (New York: Simon & Schuster, 1998).

In this highly acclaimed book, David presents the results of a study that he performed with associate Erik Lufkin, a Ph.D. in astrophysics and the director of research at the Dreman Foundation at the time, that compares relative P/Es within industry groups. Since industry sectors have some stocks that are recognized as leaders and others that are considered laggards, he compared the two segments within each industry. The most favored stocks included the 20 percent of companies in each industry with the highest P/Es. The least favored were the 20 percent of stocks in each industry with the lowest P/Es. Using this format, the highest and lowest P/Es were relative to their own industry because the P/Es in, say, technology are higher than the P/Es in the banking sector. The universe of stocks studied consisted of 1,500 of the largest companies by market size in the 27-year period between 1970 and 1996. These stocks were divided into 44 industries.

The lowest 20 percent P/E group provided a total return (dividends plus change in stock price) of 17.7 percent annually. The 20 percent with the highest P/Es provided a return of only 12.2 percent. The overall market was up 15.3 percent. Consequently, the least-favored stocks outperformed the most-favored stocks by 5.5 percent annually, while the least-favored outperformed the market by 2.4 percent. The most-favored stocks trailed the market by 3.1 percent. "To see how quickly this adds up on a compounding basis, going back to 1970 the low P/E stocks have outperformed the market by about 150 percent," he says. "Going back even further, say 40 years, and including the bubble that burst in 2001, low-P/E stocks have outperformed by an annualized margin of about 2.5 percent."

In a related study using the same universe of 1,500 stocks, David selected the top 20 percent of companies with the highest P/E and the bottom 20 percent with the lowest P/Es. In contrast to the earlier study, these stocks were not broken down by industry groups. Over the same 27-year period, the stocks with the lowest P/Es averaged an annualized total return of 19 percent, beating the high-P/E group by 6.7 percent. As expected, the low-P/E group paid dividends that averaged 6 percent over the life of the study compared to only 1.9 percent for the high-P/E group, and 4.3 percent for the overall market. Dozens of David's studies are examined in *Contrarian Investment Strategies: The Next Generation*.

Why do the high-P/E stocks underperform? David says the primary reason is that experts' forecasts are usually wrong. When providing earnings forecasts, analysts tend to be either overly pessimistic or, far more commonly, overly optimistic. In either scenario, investors will overreact, and even more investors will become attracted because investors like to follow the crowd. (David points out that there are examples of stocks that justify their high P/E ratios, just as there are stocks that deserve small multiples.)

David performed a study that examines consensus estimates among analysts going back to 1970, showing how the average estimate among all analysts missed its forecast by about 44 percent a year. Furthermore, he proves that negative surprises don't hurt value stocks as much as they do growth stocks. "The disappointments are not as earth shaking," he says. "Analyst forecasts have been very poor over time."

David has demonstrated that the odds are overwhelmingly against the investor who relies on Wall Street forecasts. His assumptions are based on a study—the largest and most comprehensive of its kind—of approximately 500,000 analysts' forecasts between 1973 and 1996 that he performed with associate Michael Berry. The nearly 8,000 consensus estimates that resulted consisted of at least four separate brokerage house forecasts, with many of these estimates having as many as 30 or 40 forecasts. On average, 1,115 NYSE, Nasdaq, and Amex stocks each quarter were part of the study. The odds of an analyst being accurate, defined by conventional Wall Street standards as being within a range of plus or minus 5 percent of the reported earning numbers, are extremely low, particularly in longer periods. "The odds are staggering against the investor who relies on fine-tuned earnings estimates," David says.

Typically, only 29 percent of forecasts are ever within five percentage points either way in any single quarter. In four consecutive quarters there is a 1 in 130 chance that earnings forecasts will be accurate; in 10 quarters, 1 in 200,000. In 20 quarters, the odds are better playing the lottery: 1 in 50 billion. Since investors do not mind if analysts are wrong on the upside, David says the odds of avoiding a negative surprise of 5 percent or more for 10 consecutive quarters is 1 in 150, and 1 in 23,000 for 20 consecutive quarters. Giving analysts far more headway did not help much either. Stretching out the range to plus or minus 10 percent of the reported earnings numbers, analysts had a 47 percent chance in a single quarter. In 4 consecutive quarters, the odds decrease to 1 in 21; for 10 quarters, the odds are 1 in 2,000; and for 20 consecutive quarters, the odds are one in four million.

Low Price/Earnings Ratio Strategies

"The inaccuracy of these forecasts shows how dangerous it is to buy or hold stocks on the basis of what analysts predict for earnings," David emphasized in his December 29, 1997 column in *Forbes*. "In a dynamic, competitive worldwide economy there are just too many unknowables for such pretended precision. This is one reason value or low-P/E strategies work: They do not depend on spuriously scientific earnings estimates. A value stock is unlikely to collapse if its quarterly earnings fall short of expectations; skepticism is already built into the price. But when earnings come in above expectations, these stocks shoot out the lights." That is because investors tend to overestimate the future of pricey, or high-P/E, growth stocks, while underestimating the prospects for low-P/E stocks.

When earnings are missed, the higher-multiple stocks can get clobbered, while the cheaper stocks show some downside protection and a bigger boost on the upside because of low expectations. "In short, surprises are often good for value stocks. Rarely are surprises good for growth or momentum stocks. With these, it's look-out-below if there's a shortfall, and a shrug of the shoulders if earnings come in on the upside."

Because of the strikingly high rate of error of analysts' forecasts, and their tendency to project on extreme levels, David believes that investors need to be realistic about the downside of an investment, and should expect the worst to be much more severe than initial projections. This is not to say that David doesn't look at any Wall Street research. While his team of research analysts continues to scour the market for values and maintain contact with companies in the portfolio, he does look at the Street's analyses. "Some of the analysts are very good," he says, "but the recommendations—or their conclusions—should get chopped off. We read the analyses, and then form our own conclusions."

Other Contrarian Strategies

In addition to looking at low P/E ratios as a contrarian strategy, David also selects stocks using price-to–cash flow (adding depreciation and other noncash charges to after-tax earnings) and price-to–book value (the value of all common stock after deducting all depreciation and liabilities). The studies comparing low P/Es and high P/Es were remarkably similar to the studies of the low price-to-book and low price-to–cash flow strategy. "All three value strategies handily beat the market and sharply outperform the best stocks in each case," he says. "These two additional strategies also offer significantly higher dividends than the overall market, and more than triple the dividend of the stocks with the higher ratios."

The fourth strategy, price-to–dividend yield, is much more controversial among traditional analysts. That's because high-dividend-paying stocks are associated with nongrowth industries such as utilities. Investors in utility stocks are seeking current income at the expense of rapid capital appreciation, whereas growth investors are sacrificing dividends for the companies' financing rapid growth. Traditional fundamental investors tend to disagree with the notion that high-paying dividends can outpace the market.

David has found that high-yield stocks outperformed the overall market by about 1.2 percent annually over the 27-year period analyzed, and beat low- or no-dividend yielding stocks by nearly 4 percent annually. However, this group underperforms the other three strategies. (All performance numbers assume that dividends are reinvested into additional shares.) "These strategies indicate that contrarian stocks can provide investors with the best of both worlds: greater stock appreciation and higher dividends," David remarks.

Value Analysis versus Security Analysis

If selecting stocks based on their contrarian attributes can beat the market over long periods of time, should security analysis be completely abandoned? "I believe parts of it can be valuable within a contrarian framework," he says. "By recognizing the limitations of security analysis, such as forecasting, one can achieve even better results within the contrarian approach. Our process is pure value analysis—we don't like dogs," he says, smiling as he begins to discuss his fundamental valuation techniques.

David supplements the contrarian methods described earlier with fundamental approaches. First he ensures that a company is in a strong financial position. "This will enable the company to survive periods of operating difficulties or economic downturns, and will help determine the sustainability of the dividend," he says. A strong financial position also helps to protect from structural flaws in the company. These analyses include sales growth, cash flow, and earnings growth, as well as evaluating a company's products.

Next, he seeks earnings growth that is faster than the S&P 500 in recent times and not likely to drop in the imminent future. He notes that this analysis is performed to estimate the general direction of earnings in the near term, and is not an attempt to forecast precise earnings. Using this valuation, David looks at Wall Street for forecasts of declining earnings, even if his analysis points the other way. "As we've seen, analysts are overoptimistic," he says. "From time to time, even forecasts of moderately declining earnings turn into nosedives." When forecasting the general direction of earnings, David is predisposed to the conservative side in order to reduce the chance of error.

Once the preceding indicators pass muster, David then determines if the company is able to sustain—and increase—a dividend yield that is greater than the S&P 500's average yield. As he proved using the low P/E, price-to–cash flow, and price-to–book value strategies, contrarian stocks can provide both higher dividend yields and greater appreciation than highly favored stocks. By seeking companies with higher-than-market dividend yields, he is able to augment the performance of the contrarian stocks. (He notes that the very highest yielding stocks will lag in appreciation versus the noncontrarian stocks, but will outperform on a total-return basis.)

The Dreman Approach

While there are variations of the strategies that can be utilized for above-market returns, David manages his investors' 11 billion dollars in assets using all four approaches—low-P/E, price-to–book value, price-to–cash flow, and price-to–dividend—plus the fundamental analyses just described. Of the four approaches, however, the low-P/E method is his core approach.

When David finds an attractive investment, he will typically sell other positions to raise cash. One of his rules of investing is to avoid unnecessary trading: "The four price-to-value strategies provide well above market returns for years; these strategies avoid unnecessary trading, thus eliminating excessive transaction costs, and enhancing portfolio returns."

He will sell a stock if its fundamentals change for the worse. "If it changes dramatically, I sell immediately," he says. "Additionally, if a stock's P/E rises above the market P/E and we can't justify holding it from a value perspective, then we'll sell—regardless of how favorable prospects may appear."

David points out that he keeps his eye on the measurement, whether it is the P/E, price-to–book value, price-to–cash flow, or price-to–dividend yield, and not on the stock's price. That is because he is measuring it relative to the market's measurement. "If we buy a stock based on its price-to–book value, and the stock triples in price, if the book also rises accordingly, it will remain equally undervalued—as long as it doesn't hit the market's price-to–book value."

For stocks that continue to look attractive according to the contrarian strategy, but whose performance has been poor, David recommends a holding period of two-and-a-half to three years, and perhaps three-and-a-half years for a cyclical stock with a drop in earnings. He advocates selling a stock immediately if the long-term fundamentals decline considerably.

In managing the Scudder-Dreman High Return Fund, he rarely has a cash position. As an alternative to relying on cash, David will hold cash equivalents, such as money-market funds, or even S&P 500 index futures to simulate full investment.

In David's opinion, the value strategies work because of analyst and investor overreactions in the marketplace. While psychology is the least-understood factor in the market, he emphasizes, it is probably the most important influencer. This is why behavioral finance is the cornerstone of his contrarian strategy.

Behavioral Finance

David and other behavioralists, as opposed to traditionalists, argue that the market is full of anomalies, and investors are driven by irrational behavior. An example of such behavior is the tendency to overreact to good or bad news, often buying or selling stocks based on little information or hunches. Another example is the inclination to consistently overvalue favorite investments, while undervaluing stocks that are out of favor. "Investors extrapolate positive or negative outlooks well into the future," David says, "pushing prices of favored stocks to excessive premiums and out-of-favor stocks to deep discounts." Consequently, companies that are expected to outperform end up underperforming, and vice versa. In effect, they both regress toward a more average valuation.

David explains further what he calls the Investor Overreaction Hypothesis. "Over long periods of time, 'best' stocks underperform the market, while 'worst' stocks outperform. Positive surprises boost 'worst' stocks, significantly more than they do 'best' stocks, and negative surprises knock 'best' stocks down far more than 'worst' stocks."

He then describes two distinct types of surprises: those triggered by events and those reinforced by events. Event triggers move the stocks' prices toward the mean; such a result would be a positive surprise on a worst stock and a negative surprise on a best stock. Reinforcing events do just the opposite; they move the stocks' prices away from the mean. Here the surprise might be negative on a worst stock and positive on a best stock. In this instance, since investors have already factored in the potential for the associated surprise, the price movements are far less than they are for the event triggers. With event triggers, because the surprise is not expected, the price movement is far greater than that of a reinforcing event. Accordingly, David adds, the greatest impact is for those stocks on the extreme ends of being a best stock or worst stock.

Other psychological reactions from investors include the treatment of losses and gains. With losses, investors display signs of regret and frustration. And when investors are losing money, they tend to hold onto a position until it breaks even. An investor will typically hold a winning trade for an extended period of time, always believing that it will continue to rise. In either case, even as the investor's expectations are that the stock will come back or keep rising, the stock typically drifts lower.

As to the overall effectiveness of his investment style, David says, quite simply, "The strategies I've developed are also backed by behavioral psychology, which is why they work. And it's far safer to project a continuation of the psychological reactions of investors than it is to project the visibility of the companies themselves."

To illustrate one of his contrarian strategies, David goes back to August 1982, when he noticed that investors and the media were particularly bearish on the stock market. This, incidentally, was only weeks before the Dow Jones Industrial Average entered a raging bull market that lifted the index ninefold over the next five years. "The negative sentiment was enormously overplayed," he says. "By many standards, stocks were trading at their lowest levels since the thirties. Investors were viewing the market as essentially dead because the index was below where it was in 1970. Consequently, investors' negative sentiment was extraordinarily high."

David and his team, taking into consideration market valuations and investor behavior, believed that stocks were in the bargain basement. "Adjusted for inflation," David explains, "the Dow was under 80, pretty close to the Great Depression lows. But book value, adjusted for inflation, was at the biggest discount to market price than at any other time since the turn of the nineteenth century." He also points out that bonds were cheaper when evaluated in inflation-adjusted, or real, terms. "The bond market had factored in all the negatives that had already happened, as well as a host of negatives that would never happen. Everyone believed it was the worst of times for the financial markets. Everyone came to the same conclusion."

Except for David and his team, who came to the opposite conclusion. David continued buying stocks and long-term zero-coupon securities, bonds that are particularly sensitive to changes in interest rates because the principal and interest are paid at maturity. At the time, headlines spelling disaster in the markets contributed to the fears. Within six months investors, like David, who recognized this major overreaction and acted on their beliefs were well rewarded: stocks and bonds started their rapid ascent, with securities such as David's zero-coupon bonds rising over 100 percent. "We believed it could be the opportunity of a lifetime for brave investors who were willing to step up to the plate."

Timing the Corrections

David offers two warnings when timing the market using his contrarian methods. "Seeing an overreaction and acting on it are two different things," he says. "Overreactions are very predictable using my guidelines, but forecasting corrections is nearly impossible."

For example, on August 24, 1987 David and his team—on record—claimed that the Japanese markets were extraordinarily overpriced and due for a fall. "The Nikkei 225 was at 25,760, and its average P/E was 86 times 1987 earnings, versus 20 at the Dow's peak in 1929, just before the market crash," he says. "Among the symptoms were absurdly high prices. To make matters worse, experts and journalists proclaimed that there was a shortage of stock, which would help to propel the market for years." This argument, David pointed out, "was also made by U.S. experts and journalists about the domestic markets in the late twenties. We also noticed that 20 to 30 percent of Japanese companies' profits were derived from trading in the stock market."

David continues, "Another sign was the notion that Japanese institutions, large holders of stock, would *never* sell. Again, we knew that was the perception of U.S. trusts in the late twenties. Lastly, so-called experts claimed the Japanese market was unique. This statement was made during every financial mania in history."

It is always better to be too early than too late. While David was accurately forecasting the depressed Japanese financial markets, the Nikkei kept rising until it reached about 37,000 in 1990. Then it started its plummet, eventually falling to a 20-year low of 7,699 in April 2003.

In 1990 the recession left financial and banking stocks at depressed levels when investors sold their holdings, fearing the worst: a nationwide banking crisis that could leave their investments worthless. David started buying that year. As usual, David invests with patience, and spreads out his purchases over time. He did not catch the financial stocks at their lows, and saw his holding fall during the last leg of the plummet. These investments dragged down his entire portfolio, posting negative returns in 1990, but still outpacing his average peer. He listened to his discipline, which told him to continue buying.

He was buying stocks like PNC, a large Pittsburgh-based bank holding company. "It was yielding 14 percent and had written off all its bad debts, but the stock went down enormously. It was cut to a third because of the fear that all banks were bad; it just got lumped in with all banks." David was buying it at around 10 dollars a share. Within a year, it hit 20; around four years later, it hit 50. Within two years, he had doubled his money on all bank purchases, and the Scudder-Dreman High Return Equity Fund was once again in the spotlight.

David then turns the discussion to Wall Street's poor timing. "I am awestruck by the phenomenon that Wall Street could be so consistently wrong, and for so long. Notice how there haven't been any long-term hot analysts; they are all short term. They tend to point in one direction, and if they hit, they are considered heroes. It is ludicrous to see these analysts make guesses, and witness so much money follow their lead. Then as soon as their short streak ends, the money finds a new analyst to follow. "Every time there's a new hot analyst, he or she is called brilliant. That is, until the streak eventually ends and investors don't speak about the analyst so pleasantly. But then they look for someone else. It seems that everyone realizes that these analysts are wrong more often than they are right, yet the crowd just continues to move together. So-called experts are wrong more often than they are right. I just hate to see so many people lose money because they're looking for someone to trust, to believe in."

Additionally, David feels that many investing pros advocate timing the market, selling when they feel the market is due for a pullback, buying when they feel the market is ripe for an upswing, and reallocating assets according to their beliefs. "Even when the timers and [tactical asset] allocators make lucky calls at the top," he says, "there is almost no chance that you will get back in anywhere near the bottom. On paper this makes sense. In the real world, it doesn't—the pros seem to judge the market direction poorly. It is widely supported by the experts that it is very unlikely that you or your portfolio manager will be able to recognize and react at the point where the market peaks or bottoms out. The same pattern shows clearly with mutual funds. Rather than supporting stocks when prices plummet, investors get trampled at the exit. When prices soar, they buy aggressively."

David feels money managers aren't immune to the herd mentality either: "Most money managers underperform the market. Over a 10-year period, a startling 95 percent will underperform the market. And yet, investors will follow the most recent hot manager, only to see him or her underperform for several years."

Technology and the Death of Value?

When the technology fever hit the markets in the mid-nineties, David never surrendered his discipline, even as the technology sector continued to climb to dizzying highs. "Value has always had its ups and downs," he says. "But I don't ever remember it being as out of favor as when the technology stocks started roaring in the mid-nineties." According to David, as the bubble continued to inflate, the more adamant investors and the media were convinced that the "New Economy" would change things forever; value was simply dead. With regard to the catastrophic levels of technology stocks, investors were saying, "It's different this time," comparing the current bubble with bubbles in the past. "People were saying, 'Value is never coming back,' " he says with a smile, shaking his head.

As one of the greatest contrarians ever, and a noted historian of the financial markets, David called the balloon ludicrous. He says that some of the values investors assigned to many dot-coms made the tulip bulb look cheap. (The increasing popularity of Holland's tulip bulbs in 1630 led to higher prices: Individuals mortgaged homes in order to participate in the fast-growing market even as prices for a single bulb soared to $20 thousand, over a million dollars in today's money. In 1637 the bubble burst, with families losing their homes and wealth.) "The valuations are absurd," he was telling investors, even as prices continued to rise. "Even though we had the best-trained generation of money managers and analysts ever, along with the best information, they contributed to investor losses of seven trillion dollars.

"This demonstrated that despite their rigorous training in establishing reasonable valuation levels for stocks, analysts and money managers could almost completely disregard time-tested standards of stock evaluation during exciting periods of technological advancements or other scientific evolutions. Investment theory does not consider that psychology plays any role in investor decision making," David explains. "In periods of mania or panic, psychological influences actually play the leading role."

David believes that a market-related crisis is the best opportunity to profit, simply because it best exemplifies manic overreaction. "In a crisis or panic, the guidelines of value disappear," he explains. "People are fixated only on prices, not on the worth of a stock. Additionally, investors will process the same information differently under varying psychological conditions. "Market experts, the media, and peers, in the belief that things will only get worse, exacerbate falling prices. And similar to reactions to a market bubble, the consensus tends to be that 'things are different,' and tips on how to deal with a catastrophe are regularly doled out."

As an example, David cites the 1987 crash, when the Dow Jones Industrial Average fell 22.6 percent, or 508 points, in a single day. "There is a natural human tendency to draw analogies and see identical situations where none exist. Many investors compared the 1987 stock market crash with the 1929 crash, because the performance of the stock market during the August through October period of 1987 was very similar to that of August through October 1929. As a result, many people jumped to the conclusion in October 1987 that another economic depression was about to occur." Instead, the market was up 22.9 percent over the next year, and two years later it was up 54.3 percent.

In *Contrarian Investment Strategies: The Next Generation*, which was written in 1996 and 1997, then published in 1998, David gave his earliest predictions for the Internet bubble. As a columnist at *Forbes*, he wrote a number of articles warning investors of a major downturn in the market. He wasn't bashful in expressing his thoughts—in the year that preceded the beginning of the technology bear market, some of his articles' titles included "Is Growth Forever?" (April 5, 1999), "Profitless Prosperity" (May 3, 1999), "Bubble-Popping Strategies" (May 31, 1999), and "Internet Myth and Reality" (July 5, 1999).

In April 1999, unperturbed by the strong markets and sticking to his convictions, David warned investors of an impending burst in the bubble. If anything, as investors continued to shun proponents of value, his contrarian mindset became far more poised. In television and print media he illustrated that companies would never reach earnings that would justify their lofty prices. He assigned the fastest growth rate of any company in American history, the most optimistic analysts' forecasts at the time, and even included highly profitable years, such as 2000 for Amazon (the company lost $1.4 billion). Then, with discounted earnings, he proved that the prices would be between one-tenth and one-twentieth the prices at which they were trading at the time.

In particular, he calculated the true values of several Internet companies versus their current values, all of which were remarkably accurate just three years later. For instance, he assigned Yahoo a real value of $16.5 versus a then-current $95 ($9.49 three years later); Qwest Communications, $12.5 versus $46 ($3.75); E-Trade, $12.5 versus $53 ($4.61); America Online, $19.5 versus $74 ($12.36). (All numbers are split-adjusted.) For purposes of his demonstration he focused on so-called blue-chip companies, and avoided the $10 billion market-cap companies, such as E-Toys, that filed Chapter 11 just months after he made this analysis.

In AOL's example, he explained how the blue-chip technology company would need 18 billion subscribers, roughly three times Earth's population, to justify the lofty levels at which it was trading in 1999. "I told investors that AOL needed to either open their service to extraterrestrials or sell out," he says. (AOL merged with Time Warner in early 2000.) At the time, he said: "The Internet companies would say that we're crazy, that they'll earn much more; after all, this is a 'New World.'" Now David says: "People have said the same thing about other speculative bubbles."

In the summer of 1999, a *Forbes* reader wrote to him: "YOU ARE A DINOSAUR who simply doesn't understand the enormous promise of the new technology stocks, particularly those on the Internet."

"A Tyrannosaurus Rex I may well be," he says with a smile, "but one that uses technology in every aspect of his life, fully aware of technology's potential. I just don't understand the colossal valuations placed on these stocks relative to even the most optimistic analysts' estimates of future earnings." He told his readers in his July 5, 1999 column: "Which side of the debate you choose could have a major impact on your portfolio in the months ahead."

Growth Stocks in Distress: An Opportunity

In contrast to other value funds, David likes to invest in growth stocks, but priced at value. "We seek to buy blue-chip stocks with solidly proven earnings growth—we don't want just cheap stock, we want growth," he stresses. "This means companies that are growing ahead of the S&P 500, and we want financial strength. Additionally, we prefer strong cash flow."

One of the best places to find these stocks, David believes, is in the midst of a sector that is depressed, or during a crisis that affects the overall market. "We look for sectors in the market that are depressed for what we believe are the wrong reasons, or if there are reasons, we'll take advantage of an overreaction," he explains. "Overreaction is one of the most predictable features of markets."

One example of an undervalued stock that has experienced an overreaction, according to David, is Philip Morris. Even though he had his last cigarette when he was in college in 1957, the stock is a longtime favorite. As his fund's biggest holding, comprising over 10 percent of assets, and around 10 million shares, the company is currently in the upper 40s, with a P/E of under 12 and a yield of over 5 percent. "Philip Morris enjoyed a nice ride over the past couple of years, doubling in price in 2000, and up modestly in 2001," he says. "Even though we've held this stock since 1988, and experienced some tumultuous times, we believe that the company's generous dividend yield and strong pricing power still provide tremendous upside potential." He points out that analysts are valuing the company at around $85 a share, so in addition to the company being heavily undervalued, David believes that "in a skittish market environment, an earnings machine such as this company is one to which investors will start to gravitate."

In regard to litigation concerns, David thinks the company's legal problems are diminishing. "These concerns have, for the most part, been lifted, with the big lawsuits behind them. However, even in the midst of litigation, the tobacco companies' enormous pricing power can easily cover any litigation-related payouts." As evidence, he notes the companies' ability to raise cigarette prices by 25 cents a pack to recoup their $250 billion settlement with the states.

He adds that two-thirds of the company's earnings come from other businesses, such as its 84 percent interest in Kraft Foods and its wholly owned Miller Brewing. Other brands include Maxwell House coffee, Philadelphia cream cheese, Country Time lemonade, Velveeta cheese, Tang, Raisin Bran, Red Dog beer, and Old English 800 Malt Liquor. David feels that "No matter what happens with the economy, people are going to buy cigarettes and food." Consequently, Philip Morris poses an attractive investment opportunity in difficult economic times. He understands why investors shun the stock because of its tobacco business, but he has not been among them. As a money manager, he keeps in mind that investors count on him for the best possible return.

Another category of overreaction is crisis investing, which David defines as extreme overreaction. "The market's reaction to the horrifying events of September 11 is one example. When it happened, investors thought people would completely stop flying, so all travel-related stocks were pummeled." At the time, David was a buyer of casino stocks, such as Harrah's. "The casino stocks got hit hard, but with their strong financial conditions and an extreme overreaction in the marketplace, we were able to buy casino stocks at very cheap levels." Within several months, David's casino positions had already doubled in price.

At the beginning of 2002, there was rampant overreaction relating to the Enron debacle, which spilled over to a number of companies whose accounting treatments may have been considered aggressive. "The market became so sensitive that the slightest whisper of an accounting irregularity at a company would send the whole market reeling.

"We buy these stocks after they've gotten hammered," he says. "We've always benefited from crises." David discusses a study he made of the 11 major crises since World War II, shown in the exhibit below. "Six were political and the other five were financial. In every case, the market was up an average of 25.8 percent after one year, and 37.5 percent after two years. In times of crises, selling is not an option-it's a time to be aggressive and buy cheap stock."

Performance of the Dow Jones Industrial Average Through 11 Major Post-War Crises

Appreciation Market	*Low After Crisis*	*1 Year Later*	*2 Years Later*
1948 49 Berlin Blockade	7/19/48	–3.3%	3.2%
1950–53 Korean War	7/13/50	28.8%	39.3%
1962 Stock Market Break	6/26/62	32.3%	55.1%
October 1962 Cuban Missile Crisis	10/23/62	33.8%	57.3%
November 1963 Kennedy Assassination	11/22/63	25.0%	33.0%
August 1964 Gulf of Tonkin	8/6/64	47.2%	3.1%
1969–70 Stock Market Break	5/26/70	43.6%	53.9%
1973–74 Stock Market Break	12/6/74	42.2%	66.5%
1979–80 Oil Crisis	3/27/80	27.9%	5.9%
1987 Crash	10/19/87	22.9%	54.3%
1990 Persian Gulf War	8/23/90	23.6%	31.6%
Average Appreciation		**25.8%**	**37.5%**

Source: David Dreman, *Contrarian Investment Strategies: The Next Generation* (New York: Simon and Schuster, 1998).

David continues: "A lot of our work is simply based on the fact that people's expectations are too high for certain stocks and equally too low for other stocks." He then makes an analogy to a bettor's tendency in a casino. "For whatever reason, people will either knowingly or unknowingly overpay—that is, lessen their odds–for certain bets, like combinations at a roulette wheel. If you continue to bet against the odds, over time you will lose. If you bet with the odds, by playing against the bettors, you are going to make a lot of money over time."

In other words, "It's all about understanding the psychology behind the markets," he explains. "Whether it's the sophisticated investor or the investor just starting out, we all make the same psychological mistakes." According to David's analyses, people are captivated by exciting new concepts, by the lure of hitting a home run, and feel comfortable forming a decision that is approved by the majority. Similarly, individuals prefer to avoid companies whose prospects seem poor. "Although the statistics drag us toward the value camp, our emotions just as surely tug us the other way," he says.

"Contrarian strategies succeed because investors do not know their limitations as forecasters," he continues. "As long as investors believe they can pinpoint the future of favored and out-of-favor stocks, they should be able to make strong returns using contrarian strategies."

Since David's first book, *Psychology and the Stock Market*, broke uncharted territory over 25 years ago, psychologists, economists, investment academics, and investors of all types are finally adopting its principles. It was his hope in the seventies that once investors saw how effective the low-P/E strategy was, and understood the reasons it worked, everyone would be following his lead. Even though scores of individuals are self-described contrarians, and there are even mutual funds that bear this name, "there are still only a few that can truly call themselves contrarians," he says. "This just means that the opportunities that I was pursuing decades ago still exist." David considers this phenomenon further proof that the strategy works; after all,

if everyone learned and followed his principles, the strategy would
be doomed.

Now that the greatest bull market in the history of the stock market
is long gone, volatility and uncertainty are at considerable levels. This
post-bull environment will certainly test the resolve of the so-called
experts, the fears of the average investor, and the success of David's
shining strategies.

CHAPTER THREE

WILLIAM H. MILLER III

LEGG MASON
VALUE
TRUST

❯ ❯ ❯

*P*ortfolio managers who outperform the stock market one year are considered successful. If they do it two years in a row, people begin to take notice. When they continue that feat for five years or longer, they often receive accolades reserved for prominent investment professionals.

And then there's Bill Miller III, portfolio manager of Legg Mason Value Trust, one of the most highly acclaimed equity mutual funds in existence today.

Few portfolio managers outperformed their respective benchmark over the past five years; over the past 12 years Bill blew away his benchmark, the Standard & Poor's 500 Composite Index, by more than 5 percentage points annually. No other investment manager enjoyed such remarkable success.

Still unimpressed? Consider this: In the 10 years ending January 31, 2003, a period that saw the best four-year consecutive advance in stock market history followed by the most painful bear market in nearly 30 years, the fund recorded an average annualized return of 16.86 percent, almost 6 percentage points ahead of the S&P 500. The fund ranked number one among all large-cap core domestic funds.

Furthermore, Bill accomplished these feats by relying heavily on a strategic value-oriented investment approach.

While Bill's success benefited shareholders, it also proved a boon to Baltimore-based Legg Mason. Bill took over the fund 13 years ago with $700 million in total assets under management. Today, Bill manages $12 billion in the fund and an additional $13 billion outside the fund.

As a result of his spectacular long-term returns, the investment community regards Bill Miller III as one of the best managers in the mutual fund industry today, and many consider him one of the greatest portfolio managers of all time.

The Seeds of Success

Bill grew up in northern Florida in the 1950s, the son of a truck terminal manager. After paying expenses each week, his father didn't have much money left over, but he put aside some to purchase stocks and he taught his ambitious son about the importance of money and investing.

Motivated by his father's interest in the stock market, Bill developed a hunger for hard work and some of his own money. By age 10, Bill mowed neighborhood lawns for a quarter a clip.

One morning, as his father perused the financial pages of the newspaper, Bill made his first inquiry about the stock market, asking about the myriad of letters and numbers that captivated his father's interest. The ensuing conversation began Bill's love affair with stocks. The manner by which investors made money impressed Bill, but the amount they could accumulate without physical labor fascinated him.

Soon after learning that the market could be fertile ground in which to build wealth, he asked his dad for advice investing his meager life savings of less than $100. Together they chose to invest in RCA. He and his father watched his investment in the communications company soar. The experience motivated Bill's ravenous interest in books on the stock market. He wanted to study the best investors and determine how they became so successful.

Through reading, Bill crossed paths with the work of legendary figures Benjamin Graham and Warren Buffett, and learned the benefits of adopting a value-oriented approach in researching and selecting individual securities.

The exceptional performance of his RCA investment increased Bill's confidence in his own investing ability. By the time he sold the stock years later, his initial investment had grown sixfold. Bill used the proceeds from the sale of RCA to purchase his first car—a sporty convertible. But Bill's drive to learn more about investing and the equity market did not end with the sale of his RCA stock.

As Bill entered Washington & Lee University, he continued to immerse himself in books on investing. Though he understood his RCA investment was impressive, he didn't appreciate how good until he read how difficult it is to outperform the market over time. Despite his burgeoning interest in stocks, Bill expanded his other interests, which led him away from strictly financial studies. He majored in economics and European intellectual history.

After graduating with honors in 1972, he took some time to travel and served a couple of years as a military intelligence officer overseas. Upon returning Bill began graduate studies in the Ph.D. philosophy program of Johns Hopkins University.

During this period, Bill's wife, Leslie, was the family breadwinner. Coincidentally, she worked as a broker at the very firm Bill would join a few years later, Legg Mason.

Bill's study of philosophy affected him profoundly. Through these studies Bill learned the importance of thinking outside the box, an ideology that many successful portfolio managers embrace in order to outperform their respective benchmarks over time. The writings of William James, a nineteenth-century psychology and philosophy professor at Harvard, particularly interested Bill. He became enamored with James's thesis on pragmatism, a major intellectual movement that began in the late 1800s.

In lay terms, pragmatism means the insistence on usefulness or practical consequences as a test of truth. Although he didn't know it at the time, Bill's intense interest in pragmatism and the great thinkers of the past helped him formulate his strategy for investing.

When not working on his Ph.D., Bill continued reading about the stock market and began to manage money. At first, he invested only family assets, but gradually he began managing money for friends, particularly those he had met in the service. For the first time, Bill had a group of investors for whom he could employ the value-oriented investment principles learned during his young lifetime. The seeds of Bill Miller's life as a professional money manager were now planted and ready to grow. Using those same basic principles, Bill manages money for thousands of investors across the country today.

The Early Years in Business

Fortunately, one of Bill's professors at Johns Hopkins University took a serious interest in him and his future. The professor, Michael Hooker, later became chancellor of the University of North Carolina at Chapel Hill. Michael knew Bill's passion for philosophy but he also realized Bill's equally strong fascination with investing. Believing he would find more satisfaction as an investment professional, Michael encouraged Bill to seek employment in finance. After serious consideration, Bill took his professor's advice and began looking for a job that could leverage his love for investing into a full-time career.

In 1977, Bill parlayed his personal investment experience and educational background in economics to land a job assisting the chief executive officer at a major manufacturer of products in the steel and cement industries. Impressed with his innate ability and work ethic, the chairman of the company eventually promoted Bill to treasurer. Among his responsibilities, Bill managed the company's investment portfolio. Overseeing the company's assets brought Bill in contact with several principals at Legg Mason, a relatively small investment boutique at that time. During this period, Bill struck up a professional relationship with Chip Mason, Legg Mason's chief executive officer.

One day during a conversation with Chip, Bill learned that Legg Mason planned to launch a new fund investing in the firm's best research ideas. Chip asked Bill if he would consider joining the firm's research team, but Bill declined. A few months later, when Chip offered him the opportunity to become the director of research, Bill accepted, officially joining Legg Mason in October 1981. Six months later, Bill helped launch Legg Mason Value Trust with then co-manager Ernie Kiehne. The portfolio's initial holdings consisted mostly of Kiehne's long-held investment ideas.

Through the years, Bill and Ernie placed heavy emphasis on accounting-based factors, such as price-to-earnings, price-to-book, and price-to-cash flow ratios. As it turned out, their discipline proved to be the best approach for selecting stocks during this particular period. As the economy emerged from a recession, the attractively priced, fundamentally sound stocks Bill and Ernie chose performed very well.

Over the next four years, the Legg Mason Value Trust's investment results trounced the competition; the portfolio recorded a performance that made this relative newcomer to the mutual fund industry the number one fund in the country in terms of performance.

Eventually the good times faded (but they did not disappear forever). The investment philosophy that had worked so well for Bill and Ernie since 1982 no longer delivered the same investment results for their shareholders by the end of the decade.

By that time, investors gravitated toward rapidly growing companies with high multiples. The outbreak of the Gulf War in 1990, followed by the first recession in eight years, created an even more perilous investment environment.

In late 1990 Ernie retired, leaving Bill to manage the Legg Mason Value Trust on his own. For the first time, Bill solely controlled asset allocation and looked forward to building a strategy that could recapture success. To this end, Bill began incorporating his philosophical studies and James's pragmatism into the investment process.

The Pragmatist Emerges

Throughout his adult life, Bill Miller's interest in philosophy rivaled his love for equities. Pragmatism interested him specifically because it is, in short, the study of that which works.

As Bill took over the fund, he began to draw more on his understanding of philosophy when making investment decisions. He viewed pragmatism as a means for looking beyond the obvious, that which was not necessarily true, and seeing future possibilities from a different perspective than most investors.

Moreover, people naturally embrace beliefs that correspond with their reality. As a true pragmatist, Bill wondered how to know when a specific methodology no longer proves successful, and why many investors might continue to embrace an ideology that no longer works. For example, many investors believe when demand for a certain product is strong and a company leads in manufacturing of that product, the price of its shares should increase because the company will benefit from high demand. As a result, the investor who bases a decision on this theory may remain invested in this company long after the stock enjoys a strong upward move and begins a period of a sustained downward trend.

By contrast, a pragmatist would stay interested in that stock only as long as the underlying company continues to prove its potential to benefit from the initial upward trend. Once that scenario becomes invalid, the pragmatist would theoretically sell that stock, regardless of what appears obvious to many others.

When Bill took over the fund, he began to depend less on expectations drawn from past series of events or carefully formulated economic and mathematical theories. Instead his process weighed the probability of something happening in the future based on the current situation. This break from reliance on backward-looking predictive analytics opened Bill to new places where accurate information might originate, even if the market did not yet embrace his probing ideology. He also embraced the emerging science of complexity theory, which meshes seamlessly with the guiding principles of pragmatic thinking.

Complexity theory is rooted in the science of energy physics dating back to the late 1800s. By the 1950s, leading economists started applying what physicists understood about how molecules work at the cellular level to complex elements that make up an economy. The physicist's molecule became the economist's rational investor, and the scientific laws guiding the behavior of those particles became business analysis.

The only hitch to this elegant mathematical theory is that economic information is far from perfect, and investors are seldom rational. By adding those variables into the equation, though, Bill has applied complexity theory to investor behavior and has come up with a unique view of investing, which proves to be a competitive advantage for his investors.

For instance, most analysts view the gaming industry as a simple balance of supply and demand. Bill takes the analysis to the next step, measuring how specific companies evolve through that landscape and asking new questions. What happens if you build more casinos in Las Vegas? If the Mirage adds 100 new rooms, is that good for Harrah's, which sits right across the street?

Along those same lines, how does Microsoft's entrance into the online market affect America Online? Can Intel ever reclaim its domination of the tech sector? Complexity theory doesn't answer these questions, Bill explains, but it opens the door to a new level of thinking and a new way of analyzing investment research.

Applying these theories, Bill determined Microsoft's vulnerability to the successful lock-in tactics America Online uses to keep its customers, so Bill loaded up on AOL. Similarly, the economic winds clearly shifted away from Intel toward low-cost competitors such as Dell. Bill bought Dell.

It all boils down to whether you believe that science is reality or whether you believe science is simply a tool that helps you cope with reality, Bill says. If you believe the former, then all scientific descriptions are either true or false. If you believe the latter, you understand science as a way to organize and make sense of our experiences.

In economics, very few things are black and white. Bill uses Manuel Johnson, former chief of the Federal Reserve, as an example. In 1993, Johnson asserted the scientific view that there was no systematic connection between high government deficits and high interest rates. Looking at bond yields vis-à-vis the deficit makes it clear that while this may be an accurate scientific interpretation of the facts, in reality the opposite is true.

For Bill, this analogy proves his point; it doesn't matter if the scientific assumptions of economic theory are true or false. It only matters if the predictions based on those assumptions become reality. This shift in thinking, coupled with extensive fundamental analytical work, set the stage for Bill to enjoy another strong round of investment performance with the fund. The Value Trust's resulting accomplishments catapulted Bill to legendary status in the world of money management professionals.

A Fundamental Investment Approach

Despite his unique perspective on analyzing data, Bill begins the research process much like most value investors. He combs the market for companies selling at large discounts to their unrealized value. The difference lies in how Bill measures that value. Most value investors just look at a company's price-to-earnings ratio, but Bill finds those numbers irrelevant when taken by themselves.

To determine the potential value of a prospective investment, Bill and his research team conduct extensive economic value analysis of all facets of the underlying company's business strategy. This research process usually involves a broad array of analytics, such as private market analysis, liquidation analysis, and leveraged buyout analysis. The team also pays careful attention to a company's ability to generate returns above its cost of capital.

In researching an individual company, Bill and his staff perform what he refers to as scenario analysis. This process examines how the business might fare in a variety of different situations. Each scenario, which includes extensive cash flow analysis over a projected time frame, gives the team a different number. The closer those numbers cluster to each other, the more confidence the team has in their projected valuation for the business. While Bill and his research team still focus mainly on price-to-earnings, price-to-book, and price-to-cash flow ratios, they realize the need to adjust the accounting metrics when events occur that change the economic landscape for a company. In the mid-1990s when the government changed the rules on how companies recorded postretirement health-care benefits on the balance sheet, price-to-book could no longer accurately describe companies whose book value dropped dramatically because of this change.

Bill and his staff push their research beyond standard number crunching to uncover value. Through continuous talks with management, suppliers, competitors, and analysts, the group builds a comprehensive picture of their investments. Bill and his team rely on their reputation as long-term investors to receive honest and candid treatment from managers. In this respect, Bill gets close to the companies in which he invests, perhaps much closer than most professional money managers. He can quickly gain a certain level of trust that other managers might take years to create with corporations. Bill's reputation throughout the business world for uncompromising attention to exhaustive research, investment expertise, and a stellar long-term performance record also helps his cause.

However, choosing investments is only part of Bill's success. His allocation strategy within a portfolio also sets him apart. The Value Trust usually invests in no more than 40 to 45 stocks, quite a low number when you consider that most equity mutual funds generally invest in 100 or more companies. This relatively focused number of holdings enables Bill and his staff to conduct in-depth research of every stock represented in the portfolio and to stay in close contact with the management of each company.

When Bill buys a stock he usually owns it for a long time. The fund's turnover rate is only 25 percent, or holding the average stock for four years, compared to 80 percent, or just over one year, for the average large-cap core fund. Bill will tell you that he hopes to own a stock forever; but as a pragmatist he quickly adds that he will hold a company for only as long as he and his staff remain confident in the underlying value and management's ability to execute its business plan effectively.

Bill allocates assets in the Legg Mason Value Trust using a simple strategy: The higher a company's potential to generate above-average investment results, the more money he is likely to invest in it. Ironically, Bill owns a lot of technology stocks, many of which have high price-to-earnings ratios compared to the market, but their relative value makes them more attractive than those in other industry groups, in Bill's opinion.

The Pragmatist at Work

Ever the pragmatist, Bill will quickly sell of a stock if he believes the company is no longer likely to keep working. On the other hand, Bill demonstrates patience with a promising company even if the share price suggests he should do otherwise. A great example is Toys "R" Us. For years Bill avoided the company, despite its very attractive appearance on paper to value managers. Its P/E ratio, price-to-book value, and historical factors all suggested a great value, but by digging deeper into the company's books and competition, Bill thought its low price was well earned.

By the early 1990s, the toy company began fixing two previous problems. Old, poorly staffed stores were getting facelifts. The company rolled out a brighter and cleaner new store prototype. It also stopped its willy-nilly expansion, focusing instead on increasing profits at existing sites. This was critical, in Bill's judgment, because the aggressive expansion was sucking up capital without producing any real returns. When the expansion stopped, management realized they held far too much inventory and cut inventory by $500 million, generating a huge amount of cash used to buy back stock.

Suddenly the equation changed for Bill. The operating strategy for the stores was back on track and the company was allocating its capital resources properly. Bill likened the makeover to the transformation that Wal-Mart went through just a few years before, so he started buying.

The same principle guided Bill and his team to Dell in the mid-1990s. Bill believed a handful of companies could join the ranks of businesses with virtual monopolies in their respective areas. Dell fit this description.

Based on his research, Bill concluded that Dell could sustain a competitive advantage over other personal computer makers even though the company's stock price—and, therefore, investor interest—did not reflect it. Bill thought most investors did not understand that as the personal computer business consolidated, a cost-conscious company like Dell would thrive in relation to its competitors.

Against this backdrop Bill invested $20 million in Dell in 1996, when the company's price-to-earnings ratio hovered in single digits. The stock rose, pushing its P/E ratio to 12, at which point many value-investment purists might have unloaded the stock. Historical valuations of personal-computer stock usually meandered between 6 and 12 times earnings. As a result, value investors moved in at the lower end of this range, and sold at the upper end.

Contrarily, Bill held his position in Dell because his macro view of the company remained valid. As a result, his shareholders enjoyed significant appreciation. In just four years, the fund's position in the Texas-based computer manufacturer ballooned 50-fold, to a cool $1 billion, making it one of the best-performing stocks of the 1990s.

How difficult was it for Bill, a true value-oriented investor, to continue holding Dell long after it evolved from a deeply discounted value stock into a growth stock with superior upside potential? He will tell you it wasn't difficult at all because Dell generated superior returns on capital and its excellent business model remained intact. From another perspective, Bill saw no fundamental reason to sell.

Yet don't think for a second that Bill eschews the importance of price-earnings ratios when selecting and deciding to keep individual stocks. Such an approach would be in sharp contrast to the beliefs of any value investor. Bill thinks that a company's price-to-earnings ratio, as well as just about any other measure of valuation, is irrelevant in isolation. Proper analysis must also consider other important factors that can indicate the potential for higher valuations.

In the case of Dell, the company had a much stronger growth rate than its major competitors. This reinforced Bill's conviction in his decision to continue holding the stock instead of selling it to purchase a more attractively priced one.

Finding Value amid the Rubble

Although Bill has made plenty of money by investing in rapidly growing companies, he has made his mark (and significant returns) by scooping up shares trading at ridiculously low valuations and selling them after they became recognized winners.

In 2002, a period when telecom stocks hit record lows, Bill increased his exposure to the downtrodden sector, focusing primarily on an existing position, Nextel Communications. When Bill stepped up his investment in Nextel Communications, he already understood the company and its strong management team, diversified product line, and solid business plan because the fund had held the stock since 1999. As of this writing, Nextel is the fund's second largest holding.

Another stock that showed up on Bill's radar during its troubled times was Tyco International. Struggling as a result of problems associated with its former CEO and corporate malfeasance, Tyco's stock came under intense selling pressure in 2002, falling to around $10 per share. After valuing Tyco's assets and realizing the company's long-term growth potential, Bill viewed the downturn as an ideal opportunity to invest heavily in the company. The decision proved fruitful. Tyco's stock nearly tripled from the middle of 2002 to the first quarter of 2004.

Buying low and selling high constitutes only part of Bill's success with beaten-down stocks. He also remains committed to these stocks once he takes a position and will even buy more shares if their valuations tumble. But Bill will continue buying a beaten-down stock far below his original purchase price only if the reasons he purchased shares in the first place remain intact.

Although Bill focuses mainly on stocks selling for significantly less than their intrinsic values, he will not let a company with strong growth prospects go unnoticed in his portfolio. The two categories are not mutually exclusive.

InterActiveCorp, formerly known as USA Interactive, the parent of such companies as Hotels.com, Match.com, Home Shopping Network, and Ticketmaster, among others, fits such a description. A dedicated follower of Warren Buffett, Bill has called InterActiveCorp "the Berkshire Hathaway of the new economy." At the time of this writing, InterActiveCorp made up more than 5 percent of the fund's holdings.

Strategy for Selling

While Bill's knack for finding value elevated him to legendary status, his sell discipline formed an integral component of his success over time. Bill will unload a fairly valued stock if a better opportunity arises or the case for investing changes. Bill and his staff consider a stock fairly valued if the underlying company is unlikely to deliver an above-average return over predetermined time horizons, usually 5 years and 10 years.

When a better opportunity arises, the fund sells the least attractive holding to make room for a company with better investment potential. The least attractive stock trades closest to its true value, as determined by Bill and his team.

Again, though, Bill follows the route of the pragmatists, not the traditional value investor. Value investors tend to be heavily influenced by historical valuation measures when buying and selling, using those measures as roadblocks. Bill uses those measures as landmarks. He looks backward at those measures, too, but places them in the context of today's environment. Is it the same environment that gave rise to the old landmark? If the answer is "yes," he sells because the stock has gone as far as it can go on this road. But if the answer is "no," Bill will take another look at the economic forces at work.

Also, the case for investing might change if a company's prospects decline as a result of a change in the tax law or a rule involving its specific business area. Though selling a security is a natural part of the investment process, Bill and his staff do hold securities in the portfolio for an above-average length of time.

A Final Word

With a track record untouched by any of his peers, it would be easy for Bill to simply rest on his laurels. But that's not the way he does things. During the bull market of the late 1990s, his portfolio, like all value funds, underperformed growth stock funds, which recorded stellar gains. Once that market bubble burst, though, Bill navigated investors successfully through what many considered to be one of the worst bear markets ever.

To this day, Bill Miller continues to employ his uniquely pragmatic approach to value investing, helping his faithful investors achieve their long-term financial goals.

CHAPTER FOUR

CHRISTOPHER C. DAVIS

DAVIS
NEW YORK
VENTURE FUND

❯ ❯ ❯

A three-generation powerhouse of investing leadership, the Davis family gives new meaning to the term "family of funds." As grandson to founder Shelby Cullom Davis, Christopher C. Davis carries on the family legacy of superior investing results, managing over $40 billion, including the $19 billion in assets in Davis New York Venture Fund and $5 billion in Selected American Shares. Posting stunning results under his leadership—the fund returned 12.88 percent over the last 10 years, 2.86 percentage points better than his average peer in his Morningstar category—he is certain to attain the same legendary status as his father and grandfather. Interestingly, each generation seems to be more intriguing than the next.

Family Values

Back in the 1940s, Shelby Cullom served as a deputy superintendent of insurance for the State of New York. He determined that even though high commissions paid to insurance salespeople diminished profits in the short run, in later years those same policies would produce tremendous cash flows. In 1947, with borrowed money, he started his own investment firm, Shelby Cullom Davis & Co., which specialized in insurance companies, along with banks and other financial institutions. The strategy seemed natural to Shelby; invest in value-rich financial companies for the long-term. At the time, the Dow staggered at 180 and Wall Street ignored insurance stocks. What he witnessed was an opportunity to invest in companies with expanding earnings, but at a price he felt was discounted. The returns were nothing short of spectacular; he turned $100,000 into more than $800 million by the early 1990s. When he died in 1994, he had led a full life as investor, author, prominent philanthropist, and ambassador to Switzerland.

His son, Shelby M.C. Davis, also considered a Wall Street legend, got started during the raging bull market of the 1960s, then successfully invested his way through the turbulent markets of the 1970s. He started his own investment firm, and initiated the Davis New York Venture Fund in 1969. Managing this fund, he outperformed the market in 22 out of 28 years. Grandsons Chris and Andrew took the reins of the Davis dynasty in the late 1980s, and continue to produce outstanding returns.

While genes had a lot to do with this family's investing legacy, so did the family's culture. For example, some vacations incorporated stops to companies for research purposes. Family dinners would likely include conversations about properly managing money, and often, thoughtful games in which Shelby M.C. would ask the boys questions designed to impress on them the power of compounding, such as "Which would you rather have, a dollar a day for 30 days or a penny that doubles every day for 30 days?" (Answer: A penny would be worth more than $5 million, versus $30.) A favorite Friday night activity for the family was gathering around to watch the television show *Wall Street Week*. Summer breaks from college were not exempt from investment experience; the boys were put to work writing research reports for $100 each.

Although it is Shelby M.C.'s firm belief that there is no substitute for hands-on experience, he strongly states that he never encouraged his sons to enter the world of investing. "If you plan that type of thing, it won't work," he says. "I wanted to teach them about stocks and how to handle their money so that even if they hired a money manager some day, they could understand investments."

Says Chris, "My father felt that the best way to get kids interested in learning, say, French, is to take them to France for two weeks. Let them see people speaking the language. Let them have a wonderful experience so that when they come back and open their textbooks, they'll really get it. I developed an interest in investing long before I had the tools; I was much more interested in acquiring the tools because I knew what the end product was all about. We were lucky enough to have been given the opportunity to explore the world on our own to determine what we really wanted out of life."

Chris was born in 1965 in New York City. After high school in 1983, he moved to Scotland to earn his bachelor's and master's degrees in theology and philosophy. While there, his interest in religion heightened, and he considered becoming an Episcopal priest. While working as a seminarian at the American Cathedral in Paris, he once asked his presiding priest, who had known him since he was a child, about his future. "When you were a child, you wanted to be a veterinarian because of your love for animals," the priest replied, referring to his volunteer work for two summers at the Humane Society. The message immediately sank in: Chris was equating helping people, making a difference in the world, with becoming a priest. "I always loved working with people, especially teaching children; the church seemed like the best vehicle for social work," he recalls. He soon realized he had an inner passion for investing, and thought perhaps this might be the best way for him to help others. Investing might indeed be his calling.

Because an informal Davis family policy states that family members can't work for the family business without first working somewhere else ("We don't want to be the employer of last resort for the family," he jokes), Chris moved back to Boston. He took a job with State Street Bank, all the while attending night classes in accounting and other related financial subjects. Then he spent several years as a financial services analyst at Tanaka Capital Management and took courses at the College of Insurance. Chris's father and grandfather discouraged him from pursuing an MBA because they felt it teaches investors to think alike. However, they believed accounting was necessary when scrutinizing companies.

On Saturdays Chris wrote two-page newsletters on investing in insurance companies for his grandfather's research company, which sent them out to investors. After writing the newsletters and stuffing them in envelopes for several months, Chris noticed that many of the recipients no longer lived at the listed address, and many weren't even alive. Additionally, he realized there was no financial benefit to the company; they weren't receiving fees for writing the newsletter or for providing research. His grandfather summed it up: "We do it for ourselves—discipline," he told Chris. Chris continued to write the newsletters, and that is one reason why he takes great care in writing the commentaries himself in his mutual fund's annual reports.

Continuing the Tradition

In 1991 he joined his father's investment management business. To prove he had what it took to invest, he started the Davis Financial Fund so he could quantify his results. He chose this discipline for two reasons: The financial industry was the sector he knew best, and it was directly related to the Davis New York Venture Fund, which he aspired to one day manage. He got off to a running start: In his first three years running the Fund, he outperformed both his peers and the S&P 500 by wide margins. Indeed, he had proved to the world that he could carry on the family tradition of producing outstanding investment results.

In 1994, at the age of 29, he was made the primary manager for the New York Venture Fund and its no-load companion, Selected American Shares. (In 1998, Kenneth C. Feinberg was added as Chris's co-manager for both funds.) His father, Shelby, is research advisor, and brother Andrew manages the Davis Real Estate Fund and Davis Appreciation and Income Fund.

Chris learned a great deal about his grandfather's and father's investment philosophy while he was writing the newsletters. "My grandfather loved to find what he called growth stocks in disguise," Chris says, referring to stocks of a company whose earnings stream is poised to grow at a faster rate than what investors were expecting, "or to find a company whose earnings are growing at a value price."

"My grandfather also coined the term Davis Double Play," he adds, "taking the growth stock in disguise one step further by providing the best of both worlds: finding a growth stock in disguise, plus realizing a price-to-earnings multiple expansion as investors appreciate the growth opportunities and bid up the stock. His goal was always to get the double play.

"It makes a lot of sense," Chris continues, "because if you are wrong on the rising price-to-earnings multiple, but you are right on the earnings, you can still do well." When considering stocks for the double play, Chris prefers stocks at growth rates between 8 and 15 percent "because these rates are easier to sustain. My grandfather used to say that he wants to invest in the doers, not the bluffers. He felt that the trouble with paying 30 times earnings for a 30 percent growth is that it is not going to grow 30 percent for long. The trouble starts when the growth rate slows, and you witness a lower estimate of future earnings coupled with a lower multiple on those low earnings, a term he called the Big Loss. The Big Loss is the opposite of the Double Play. Sort of like compression.

"The belief is that you can turn a steady, decent, but unremarkable growth rate into a wonderful stock return if you have discipline about how much you paid for it, with the added benefit of reducing the potential for getting the Big Loss.

"My grandfather and father both felt that one of the best opportunities to find the double-play combination, historically, have been in financial stocks. For whatever reason, they observed, the financial industry always sells at a discount. Maybe it's because of the companies' tendency to use leverage. It's a commodity business. There are always some bankruptcies occurring. It's cyclical. Or maybe it's because Wall Street analysts don't like to recommend other securities firms to clients. But then again, some of the greatest growth companies of the last 20 or 30 years are financial companies, like AIG and Berkshire Hathaway.

"It's pretty amazing that 20 years ago Citibank was one of the largest companies in the world, and it still is. Why? It's because money compounds on itself and, as I learned that in the insurance industry, it's not an industry where people get out of Wharton Business School and say, I want to get into insurance. The insurance industry tends to attract less competition, so there's an opportunity for a great manager in a great company in the financial world to be like a fox in the hen house. Most financial services companies also have no limits on growth. In other industries, companies are going to sell only so many baskets or cars. So many companies are limited not only as to how much they can make of a certain quality, they're limited also as to the size of the market. And if they were five times larger than they are now, they wouldn't be in the business. The business would have to significantly change. Once it changed, it might have to become a commodity business; if it became a commodity business, it would take a whole different skill set. You'd have to have somebody running it that was fierce on costs, and on sourcing material in China.

"Now, if the same fellow ran an auto insurance company," Chris continues, "he might determine that by going direct to customers instead of going through insurance agents he could save customers 10 or 15 percent. Now, if the average policy is $1,200, that means they are saving $100 or $180. That's a big difference. And by the way, the type of people who would be interested in saving $180 on their auto insurance and go through that process of calling the number to discuss the savings are probably going to be more conservative people. So you're actually going to have people who are probably more honest, who are certainly more careful because if they are prudent in that aspect of their lives, chances are they drive a Ford Taurus. That is a stunning insight! What's more, this business is scalable. Having been one of the best growth companies in America for the last 20 or 30 years, the most successful company in the country doing this is Geico, which incidentally has only 4 percent of the market (Geico is wholly owned by Berkshire Hathaway, which is a top-10 holding in the Davis New York Venture Fund portfolio). So there's no end to how much that can compound. How big can a big investing house get? Due to its scalability, its size is almost unlimited. That's the power of compounding.

"This is a philosophy that can apply to any company. For example, consumer product, technology, or energy companies could present opportunities to buy great growth rates for low prices. My grandfather believed that the philosophy applied most aptly to financial companies, so that's where he primarily invested."

Chris points out that his father would invest in any industry to reflect macro trends. "We had enormous holdings in natural resource companies and fertilizer companies," Chris says. "The eighties showed a massive shift toward consumer companies. In the seventies it was real estate, when the baby boomers were starting to buy houses. In the eighties, they were starting to have kids. They've got to buy all those consumer brands—the Campbell's soup and the Quaker Oats—and all of those consumer brands were considered consumption companies as they entered their peak spending years. In the nineties they moved into their peak savings years, and that's where they still are. Consequently, we've had this decade of strong financial companies. Now, if you had stayed invested in one sector during those three different periods, you probably didn't do very well."

When Chris seeks investments, ideas are either generated in a top-down approach, like looking at broad themes, such as the interests of baby boomers, or bottom-up. For bottom-up ideas, he will look at beaten-up stock prices or management acumen.

Buying Business, Not Stocks

Chris gives credit to one of his long-time heroes, Charlie Munger, Vice Chairman of Berkshire Hathaway, when describing the process of narrowing down a stock. "The whole investment process is really reduced when you consider stocks as businesses; this way, the process boils down to just two questions. They are the same questions you would ask if you were going to buy a business—any business. The first question is: What kind of business do you want to own, or what should be the characteristics of the type of business that you want to own, thinking in terms of a private business?

"Warren Buffett once posited that if you imagine you inherited some money but it came with the stipulation that you had to invest it all in one business and you could never sell, what are the sorts of characteristics you would look for in that business? When considering what kinds of businesses you want to own they are probably ones that either earn a high return on capital or have the potential to do so. In short, you want it to be a good business financially. That's a quantitative measure. But it's not an easy quantitative measure. People say, oh, you just screen for a return on invested capital. No. That's garbage in, garbage out analysis. In other words, the numerator, being the return, must be adjusted. Just the way you would with a private business. Thinking about it another way, if you ran a private business and you kept the books, you would report to the tax authorities what your income is. This would pose certain questions for you. You would make a lot of choices that would involve legitimately reporting income as low as possible. You would put up reserves for some items, you would defer revenue, and you would expense things that you might otherwise capitalize. All those things would serve to lower your return—I am going to come back to this when we talk about owner earnings. But, when you look at return on capital, you want that numerator to be the real return, not the reported return, not the taxable return, but what the owner return is. Then you've got to know how much capital is really required to run the business versus how much happens to be historically invested in the business so you can make adjustments accordingly.

"The second question you would ask when looking for a business, whether it's a big insurance company, consumer products company, or another company, is that if it is a good business or it has the potential to be a good business, why would those high returns be competed away? Because we live in a capitalist society. If there are high returns, capital will flow into competitors that will compete for the business.

"That's when you start looking at sources of competitive advantages. Does the company have brands? Does it have patents? Is it a market share leader? Is it a market share gainer? Is the current managing team just particularly smart? What is it that allows them to earn a high return and what makes you think that return will be sustainable?

"Remember, as in this example, you are stuck with that business because you are an owner. If it is a dry-cleaning business that is wonderfully profitable, you are going to want to make sure that a rival can't open next door. What can you do to prevent that from happening? Maybe you open one down the street to obtain critical mass so that it would be harder and harder for another establishment to compete. Maybe you charge low prices and you keep your costs so low that you are always deferring the great returns.

"The next point to consider in our business analogy assumes that although you are going to own this business, you are not going to run it—who are you going to hire to run it? Do you trust them to keep the books? Do you trust them to understand the sources of competitive advantages?"

Chris turns to the next crucial aspect of selecting a stock, again thinking in business terms. "How much do you pay for it? Remember, it's very possible to overpay for a wonderful business only to see it turn into a lousy investment. Going back to the dry-cleaning business example, let's assume it makes $100,000 a year and there's a likelihood of that increasing at twice the inflation rate. If you could buy that business for, say, $500,000, it would be a wonderful investment. If the owner decides to sell you the business, but it's going to cost you $5 million, you would say that's a terrible investment because even though it's going to grow— even if it's going to grow forever—you might reap better gains from a bond than buying this business. If it's a million dollars, you might say, well, that looks pretty good. If it were $2 million, you'd have to model it out. Again, you've got to model it out against your obvious alternative, which is a risk-free government bond. That should always be the hurdle that you have in mind."

Here Chris returns to the cost of ownership with a more intricate, but realistic, example. "The slightly more complicated version involves three steps. First, you are going to determine how you would be paying for the business. In the dry-cleaning example, if the owner says he's going to sell it to you for a million dollars, you might say that sounds terrific. But he may have overlooked a building mortgage for $900,000. And suppliers might be owed $300,000. Because you will assume those liabilities when you buy the business it may not look so attractive. Alternatively, the owner might tell you that the cost includes the entire block of real estate, which is on the balance sheet at cost for $200,000, which is what was paid for it 25 years ago, but he feels it's now worth $2 million. In this scenario, you will pay a million dollars and receive $2 million worth of real estate that is on the balance sheet at cost, which is appropriate.

"Or the owner may say that he's depreciated all of these machines and a large investment must be made to buy new ones. If you buy the business, you may only have one year left on the machines. In this case, you must first adjust the balance sheet. How much are you really paying? Are assets or liabilities inappropriately valued on the balance sheet due to varying accounting conventions?

"Next to be considered is the return of capital," Chris says. "You want to understand how much the business is really earning. Of course, the owner knows how much it's really earning. But remember, he might be recording one set of figures to the tax authorities and one set of figures to his investors, because there's GAAP (generally accepted accounting principles) earnings and there's taxable earnings. For taxable earnings, you choose every accepted accounting policy that depresses income. When reporting GAAP earnings, it may be the opposite; you may choose every accounting policy that makes your current income look as high as possible because CEOs have, unfortunately, become obsessed with the short-term. This leads to capitalizing items that really should be expensed, and upfronting revenue that you should be deferring, and issuing stock options because you don't have to put them on your income statement.

"The end result of these adjustments is a number that we call 'owner earnings.' It's going to reflect all these items: We are going to try to normalize tax rates; we are going to try to normalize interest costs; and most importantly, we are going to normalize depreciation and amortization. Going back to the dry-cleaning example, the owner may say these machines are going to last another two years, and the new machines cost three times as much with the same capacity. If this occurs, the earnings of the business might decrease because you're going to invest in new and expensive machinery that will have to be depreciated as a cash expense."

A look of frustration appears on Chris's face, and he says: "It's like EBITDA [earnings before interest, taxes, depreciation and amortization]. Whenever you hear somebody say EBITDA, cover your wallet because depreciation is a real expense. As a real expense, you have to pay it up front. Depreciation expenses can be understated or overstated; this is a very important item to focus on." Chris then offers a definition of owner earnings. "Owner earnings is the amount of cash that the business generates after appropriately reinvesting to maintain a competitive position and adjusting for all accounting policies to get to a conservative assessment before investing for growth."

That said, Chris turns to the third part of valuation: "What will the business do with the earnings? Your manager could pay out the earnings as a coupon—or dividend—payment on your capital outlay. Or he may choose to open another store on the next block, and maybe one more down the street.

"Alternatively, he may decide to buy out your competition at 30 times earnings so he can be the grand fromage of dry-cleaning," he says with a laugh. "In this scenario, even though you paid the right price you might be concerned that the business returns will be diluted by poor reinvestment of the owner earnings." Chris refers to these investing opportunities for the earnings to be the reinvestment rate on the coupon.

Buying Value and Growth

These different scenarios, Chris says, represent the differences between the value investors and the growth investors. "The value people are focused on how much they pay for the equity, and how much the business is currently earning—what are the adjusted assets and liabilities and how much is it making today? They're not as concerned about the reinvestment rate or the quality of the business.

"The growth guys," Chris says, "are primarily interested in the reinvestment rate, often without regard to whether growth rates are sustainable. So they look at a growth rate, but disregard the time element—how long it will last." Chris then describes the PEG ratio, or price-to-earnings multiple divided by growth rates, as "nonsense, because mathematically they are leaving out a key element of the equation." For example, if one buys a stock growing at 30 percent for 30 times earnings, it is considered an attractive investment for the next 10 years. "In fact, I would pay 50 times earnings if a company could sustain that growth rate for 10 or 15 years. But, if it only grows 30 percent for four years, your investment is very poor. The 'how long' part of the equation is mathematically crucial, but many growth investors don't give much attention to this variable."

In looking at individual stocks, Chris has a bias toward large-cap companies, as it is difficult to find small companies that have proven records and global leadership. "Although we occasionally uncover smaller companies with such characteristics, they are more of a rarity. We have such a strong interest in the durability of a company that we just naturally tend toward larger companies." Chris also has a bias toward high-quality companies that can grow but is quick to point out that "although our goal is always to buy such companies, it is important to realize that when we buy a company, it might not be perceived as high quality or as growing. In fact," he says, "we are often looking at companies when they are under a cloud, suffering short-term setbacks or surrounded by controversy."

Sounding like his grandfather, he continues, "Our goal is to buy what we call 'growth companies in disguise.' In this way, we hope to benefit from the double play of growing earnings and an expanding valuation." Unlike traditional deep-value investors, Chris prefers companies with great economics and good growth rates. "We try never to buy a company that we think will be smaller in five years. We focus on the future more than the present and try to look at how dramatic changes can produce huge cash flows in a business that may not be earning very much today. "For decades, fortunes were made owning television broadcasting companies that generated huge cash flows but, because of the vagaries of GAAP accounting, had very little reported net income." Chris invested in the cellular companies in the 1990s for the same reason. "Although by traditional value measures, they looked expensive, our analysis of the growth and the monopoly characteristics of owning licenses led us to conclude that the companies were really great values despite appearing superficially expensive." In this way, Chris considers himself a bit of an omnivore, willing to at least consider many types of companies that other value investors would simply rule out.

Chris believes that this view is commonsense in other areas of investing. "If you were buying a private company, you would obviously recognize that a company that grows profitably is more valuable than one that does not grow. If you were buying a shopping center, you would pay more if it were located in a fast-growing area than if it were located it an area where population is shrinking. But in the world of stock investing, managers are expected to stay in specific style boxes. The result is that there is a category of managers that place no value on growth and another category that places no limit on growth. Both seem to be looking at only part of the equation."

Thinking Outside the Box

When seeking value situations, Chris often looks at the worst headlines. "That's where the real depressed prices can be found," he says, but cautions: "Often a decline in prices doesn't automatically mean that there's value, because the businesses can deteriorate faster. You want to focus on the businesses in which you have some conviction will still be functioning 5 or 10 years from now, businesses that you can really understand." This philosophy also refers to the market in general.

"I'm reminded of my grandfather's words here. He said, 'You make most of your money in a bear market, you just don't realize it at the time,' because you're able to buy good businesses at cheap prices. And although it doesn't feel good because of the uncertainty, this is when the opportunities are best." Chris displays a historical chart of the S&P 500 and asks rhetorically, "What were the two best years for the S&P 500 in the last 30 years?" He answers: "1995 and 1975—both years it was up over 37 percent. Interestingly, people consider the time period from 1966 to 1982 as a dead market, with no good headlines," referring to the Dow Jones Industrial Average closing around 1000 in 1966 and not closing above that number again until 1982—a time period marked by events such as Vietnam, high inflation rates, and OPEC conflicts. "But meanwhile, it was going like this," he says, mimicking the index on the chart by moving his index finger up and down. "In 1976 the market was up 25 percent, and in 1980 it was up 32 percent—in the five-year period from 1975 to 1980, there was a powerful bull market that returned about 18 percent a year. I remember the cover of *Business Week* magazine, August 13, 1980, titled 'The Death of Equities.'"

He continues by explaining risk versus the perception of risk in the markets during turbulent times. "For example, we all feel that flying is riskier now than it was before 9/11. Of course, prior to the tragic events, risk was far more dangerous; we were just unaware of the potential risks. So this knowledge of the risks has created a sense that it's more dangerous when, in fact, it's actually safer. This doesn't mean it's completely safe, but it's certainly safer than it was before the event—we're more aware, there's more security, and so on. So the perception of risk has reduced the risk.

"It's the same way with investing. Investing in 2002 felt awful. It also felt awful after the crash in 1987. Nobody wanted to invest. These were great times to find values in the market. Now, conversely, back in March of 2000, there was a sense that investing was a very low-risk activity, with the expectation that the long-term annual return on equities would be 15 percent or higher. Yet, the risks were greater. Tyco is a great example. Investors were piling in at $50 a share, and piling out at $8. Whatever ends up with Tyco, it was certainly a far less risky investment at 8 than it was at 50."

Chris points out that over a 19-year period, from 1984 to 2002, the average equity mutual fund returned about 10.2 percent, but the average investor in equity mutual funds earned a paltry 2.6 percent. How does this compute? He describes it as the cost of switching. "Investors were timing the market, and they were wrong. While some mutual funds returned stellar results, the number of investors who actually attained those results were few."

This is one reason Chris feels an important part of his job is to keep shareholders in his mutual funds invested during times of underperformance. Likewise, during times of overperformance, he won't enthusiastically market the fund because he doesn't want investors to get in at the wrong time.

Always Learning

Chris is most proud of the culture at the Davis organization—one that is devoted to servicing investors; one that takes pride in its successes but readily admits its mistakes. In fact, in a walk down the corridors of the Fifth Avenue headquarters in New York City a visitor may see displays of a number of successful investments, whereas a reminder of several mistakes may be found on the wall in the research department. "We really want an environment where people are sort of jumping over themselves to take responsibility for mistakes, so we frame them. We put up plaques that describe what we did wrong and the lessons we've learned. Then we place the plaques someplace where we will look at them every day. You see," he continues, "we are going to make more mistakes—we just don't want to keep making the same ones. This is an environment in which we openly discuss our mistakes, and learn from them."

Chris's face lights up when he speaks of the firm's research capabilities, particularly as represented by the people. An excellent staff is crucial to the firm's stellar track record because it doesn't rely on Wall Street research. Nor does the firm hire from Wall Street, instead bringing in those who can add value in creative ways. For example, Chris's co-manager, Ken Feinberg, has deep experience in the insurance industry. One individual was an investigative journalist; another individual holds a Ph.D. in music; another ran a specialty chemical operation for Amoco; and one was a consultant at Bain & Co. And of course, Chris always speaks highly of his father: "He's an incredible resource; we would be crazy to make any investment without talking to him first."

When asked about his best investment, Chris politely says he would rather discuss his worst investment. "Lucent," he says without hesitation, pointing to a plaque. "Our biggest mistake in terms of dollars and cents, but also the biggest cultural mistake. It reminds me of Three Mile Island in the sense that the warning systems worked, but the operators kept overriding them. Same with Lucent. These flags would be raised from our discipline, but we would sort of manually override them because we were so convinced that it was a wonderful company, one of the most admired companies in America."

When asked about other investments on the wall, Chris reveals that many were mistakes even though the firm made money on them. "They're on the wall because we were just lucky to make money," he says more seriously. "We were wrong in our analysis. We were wrong in our assessment of their stream of coupons. We were fundamentally wrong in our assessment of the character of the people investing those coupons for us." Then he points to another frame: "Or we were fundamentally wrong in assessing the strength of the balance sheet."

Chris believes that the information available to investors can be detrimental when they form their own judgments based on headlines. He continues, pointing to more plaques: "We bought Citicorp when headlines were saying they were going bankrupt. We were buying California savings and loans when Wall Street avoided them. We bought Salomon Brothers at the peak of the Treasury scandal; American Home Products during the Fen Phen litigation; Philip Morris at $18 a share in 1999 when people thought they were going to go bankrupt—the list goes on and on. When the bad news is in the headlines, chances are we are going to be interested. Hopefully, we don't already own it, but often we will be buying it next."

Chris feels that window dressing, or the act of buying or selling shares in a mutual fund near the end of a quarter in order to improve the appearance of the portfolio before it is disseminated to clients or shareholders, is a recipe for disaster. "This is done because quarter-end holdings are published, and managers want investors to feel good about what is in the portfolio so they sell the losers and buy the stocks that have been going up. The managers are then holding stocks they don't believe in—it just seems too dishonest."

Pointing to a letter in his pocket, Chris states that it is from an angry investor who asks why the portfolio is holding a telecom company. Chris, who has significantly outperformed the benchmark indexes for three straight years—which included the telecom holding for part of the time—says that he is working on a response. "We are always going to have tortoises and hares, because we prepare for all scenarios in the market. We don't know if we are in the recovery, or in the beginning of a deep bear market. We just don't know. So we are going to try to run the portfolio for all weathers. This means that the portfolio is never going to be optimized to the current conditions. I'm sure that in the short term we will be crushed by aggressive growth investors or deep value investors. I don't know which. But if we can beat them both over five years, that would be an achievement.

"Additionally, we are always trying to plant some seeds, harvest some fruit and pull some weeds with a low turnover approach. We just don't understand how someone can manage a portfolio with 100 percent turnover. (A turnover rate of 100 percent indicates that, on average, every stock in a portfolio is bought and sold within one year.) Why bother having a research department? With high-turnover investing, you aren't investing in businesses, you are speculating about psychology. An investor can be very successful doing that; it's just a different business. It's speculation versus investing. As they say, 'in the short-term the market is a voting machine, but in the long-term it's a weighing machine.' " (The Davis New York Venture Fund's average turnover is around 15 to 20 percent, versus over 90 percent for the average equity mutual fund.)

Investing with Conviction

When pushed for his best investment story, Chris respectfully defers to one of his favorite stories—when he bought Costco, the membership-based stores that offer members low prices on a wide range of merchandise, in early 2000. "It is a wonderful business," he says. "Generally we don't own retailers, but Costco is peculiarly different because of its membership structure. Its model is very difficult to duplicate. Nothing that they sell is marked up more than 14 percent, and their net margins are unbelievably low. In fact, the money that they make on memberships is where the real profits are.

"It is also the membership structure that makes the business so unique. First, with this structure, consumers don't steal from you. Shrinkage is a big expense for most retailers. Not so at Costco. Thieves don't give you their driver's license or credit card numbers, get their picture taken, then pay you $50 and go inside and steal. Even if they did, what would it be, a pallet of toilet paper? Second, because they pay the fee, members want to take advantage of their affiliation frequently, and they feel comfortable knowing that the store isn't going to try to squeeze more money out of them, almost like a bond of trust. Costco is effectively saying, 'there's nothing in which you are paying greater than 14 percent more than what we paid for it.'

"We watched this company's stock for years, but refused to pay any price for the sake of owning it. In fact, there are a lot of companies that we admire, where we go to their meetings, visit their stores, meet the management. But there's no way we can force the math to work. With Costco, we were looking at the stock as it rose from 35 into the 50s in early 2000. Then there was some grumbling that they were going to miss a quarter, and the stock dropped from 55 to 50. Then to the mid-40s. Then they announced that earnings would be lower than expected, and the stock opened at $29.

"I heard the news on the radio early that morning when Ken walked in the office and said, 'Chris, did you see Costco missed their numbers? We might really get a shot here.' Then my dad called from the shoulder of the Massachusetts Turnpike and said, 'I just heard on the radio that Costco missed. Do you think we'll get a shot?'

"We immediately started researching why the company missed their earnings forecast. 'What was going on?' we asked ourselves. We found out that they were opening more stores than expected because they were obtaining higher returns in the stores. The new stores take six months to enter profitability, so that depressed the news. They switched to the American Express card from the Discover card as the only card they would accept. As a result, the interchange fee would be slightly higher. Even though the market saw this as a negative, it really meant that people were spending more money, and there would have to be a cost associated with it. Another part of the depressed news: They built two extra supply warehouses to make them more efficient; these would be expensed in the current quarter.

"If I were running a private business, those are all steps I would take. We thought it was wonderful. We knew that our price target was now in the mid-30s. Then the stock opened at around $29 a share. That day, we bought 17 million shares at an average price of $29. We became the largest shareholder within the period of a single day."

While Chris has had his share of "10 baggers," or stocks that rise in price by a factor of 10, to him the Costco investment represents the right approach to initiating a position in a company. Costco was first recognized as an outstanding business by Chris and the research team, unique in its approach to retailing from other traditional retailers. Second, the investment represents the discipline of waiting for the appropriate price. "When we look at a potential investment, we calculate a range of fair values we feel the stock is worth," he says. "It can be a pretty wide range, as high as 50 percent or more. For example, we could think fair value is between 20 and 50 on a particular stock. In the case of Costco, we thought it was between 35 and 50 at the time. If a company is in that range or higher, we aren't going to buy it. If we own it, we aren't going to sell it because it's somewhere in fair value."

While Chris tends to hold companies well over five years on average, he will sell if one of three reasons emerges. "One is that the fundamentals of a business deteriorate and aren't likely to improve," he says. "The second is loss of trust in the management. The third reason would be if a stock's price rises to a point beyond what we call fair value, where the valuation is beyond the growth rates in which we are comfortable."

The fund's biggest holding is American Express, at over 6 percent of assets. "We love the company's powerful global brand in both the small- and large-business area through their corporate card, the consumer card, its savings business, and its American Express Financial Advisors business. With the credit cards, the company owns both the merchant relationship and the relationship with the consumer, and earns a higher interchange fee as a result. Additionally, their customers tend to behave rationally knowing that they need to pay the entire balance off every month."

Risk is inherently managed through Chris's approach to investing in up and down markets. "Any time we make an investment, we ask ourselves, 'How much can we lose?' Only then do we consider the upside potential.

"Additionally, the types of securities we buy help us to manage risk because they are typically strong companies that are bought at distressed prices. Buying undervalued companies helps reduce risk because the prices are already beaten to the point that we consider them cheap; if things don't work out as we planned, their prices are less likely to fall than in the case of other companies that might be purchased at fair value or at a premium."

Managing Money with Pride

Perhaps what makes the Davis funds so unique is the consideration shown to shareholders in terms of governance. "We all have an invested interest in making the right decisions," he says, referring to the governance of the funds. Collectively, the Davis family, employees, and directors are the largest shareholder, with $2 billion invested alongside their clients out of the more than $40 billion under management. "Perhaps many managers would manage the portfolios as if it's their money and avoid stupid acts, like window dressing, or take more appropriate risks and not swing for the fences for so many trades. I just believe that you tend to handle your own money differently; this is how we handle the money for all of our investors. We view our jobs as stewards of capital for the long term.

"We care about building something that we can be proud of," Chris says with a serious look on his friendly face. This is really important to us. We walk in the doors every day seeking to add value for our investors, trying to be the best managers possible over a long period of time. This is why it means so much to us when we get letters from shareholders thanking us for enabling them to send their children to college, or retire comfortably. This is our greatest return."

PART II

, , ,

Mid-Cap Mutual Fund Managers

CHAPTER FIVE

JOHN CALAMOS

CALAMOS
GROWTH
FUND

❯ ❯ ❯

*W*hen John Calamos was 17, he invested his parents' savings of $5,000 in five stocks. Under his management the portfolio grew over time, and his parents were able to use that nest egg for retirement. This story seems to be the norm for John, not an isolated incident in which he was able to change people's lives. After all, as the most successful mid-cap growth mutual fund manager in the business—and one of the all-time-best managers—he has had the opportunity to help hundreds of thousands of individuals reach their dreams, too. In the 10-year period ending December 31, 2003, the fund returned an annualized 20.6 percent, far surpassing its benchmark, the Russell Midcap Growth Index, by 11.2 percentage points, and exceeding the S&P 500 index by 9.54 percentage points. The Calamos Growth fund was easily ranked number one among its peers during this timeframe.

Family Values

Growing up in an ethnic family on the West side of Chicago in the forties taught John the meaning of family, extended family, and individuals with like interests contributing to a goal of prosperity. After emigrating from Greece, John's father settled in Chicago and started a business: a local Greek family grocery store, which also housed the Calamos family on the floor above. In a typical family evening after business hours they would often reopen the store several times in a single evening so a father could pick up a gallon of milk or butter for another family. There was nothing that a customer was not entitled to, even if it was four o'clock in the morning and the local newspaper boy was hollering upstairs for some bread. The senior Calamos was also a friendly bank, lending money or groceries until payday. "My father really took customer service to a whole new level," John says, thinking back. His mother and father's example instilled in him a strong work ethic; he doesn't remember a day when the entire family was not involved in running the grocery store.

One day, while taking inventory, John stumbled upon several stock certificates, which had evidently been stored immediately following the Depression some 15 years earlier. The 15-year-old's eyes saw a gold mine, hoping it was enough to save his family from hardships for the rest of their lives. After some investigation—and not wanting to share the secret until he knew the value—John realized that the certificates were worthless. But what he did come away with was a fascination for the financial markets. As his father had found business freedom when he came to the States, John realized the power of the free markets and the ability of individuals to collectively take ownership and collectively prosper. "Growing up, I decided that I would spend my life doing interesting things," John remembers. "One of those things was investing."

Studying finance came easy to John, and his interests in the financial markets intensified. That is when he encouraged his parents to let him invest their money. "I distinctly remember thinking to myself, 'God, I wish I would have started this 10 years earlier; I missed the big up market!'" he says with a smile. Among the stocks he bought were seven shares of Texas Instruments, and shares in Beckman Instruments and Thiokol Chemical. He put the same amount of money into each stock. At this point in his recollection, John laughs, and describes the first and last tip he ever took: "My cousin told me the company Muntz TV was going to take off. The stock promptly went belly-up. I learned a big lesson—money is a valuable commodity; always do your own homework."

Finding His Way

John earned an undergraduate degree in economics at the Chicago-based Illinois Institute of Technology by working and participating in the ROTC program. After receiving his MBA in 1965, he proceeded into the Air Force, and spent five years on active duty with a tour in Vietnam. "My military service was really the first time I got out of Chicago, let alone fly in an airplane," he says. The 23-year-old was anxious to fly; it was an adventure of which he had always dreamed, and it was better than the alternative: returning to West Chicago and working as a factory foreman. "Flight school was very intense," he says. "I literally went from never being in a plane before to flying supersonic jets in formation less than one year later. That year was a phenomenal experience; it was demanding and enjoyable, and it toughened me up mentally."

In Vietnam, John flew as a forward air controller, earning a Distinguished Flying Cross and 28 Air Medals. After five years active duty and rising to the rank of major, he spent 10 years flying fighter jets in the reserves. John remembers thinking to himself as he was in combat that nothing could be more difficult. "I realized that every second I was out there, an enemy was trying to kill me. I knew that when I returned to the States, nothing could be that difficult." John also remembers the strict mental discipline he developed in the armed forces, particularly flying planes. "You can't fly airplanes for a long time without having a lot of things go wrong," he says. "Between maintaining the planes in top-notch condition and keeping mentally tough to avoid being shot down, I learned a lot about risk. I spent a lot of time thinking about controlling and managing risk. There's an old saying, 'There are old pilots and bold pilots, but no old, bold pilots.' There are a lot of parallels to investing. And of course there's the discipline, always living life by checklists and schedules."

When he returned to the States, the fighter pilot was stationed in Minot, North Dakota, flying B-52s. "We were fully prepared for World War III, flying planes loaded with nuclear weapons," he says. When John was not flying planes, he was sitting in the "hole," studying finance—in particular, convertible securities.

Developing a Strategy

Eager to begin a career as an investment professional, John became a stock-broker. While other stockbrokers were complaining about the recession and the poor performance of the markets, John was optimistic; after all, if this was the worst of times in the market, it would not even compare to Vietnam. What differentiated John from the rest of the brokers was his ability to manage risk—the biggest lesson he learned in war.

He developed a convertible hedging strategy, which included buying convertible bonds and shorting the underlying stock or writing options against the underlying stock. This strategy worked well in the high-inter-est-rate environment when stock prices were depressed. In other words, the convertible bonds—bonds that pay interest and can be exchanged for a specified number of common shares—were paying relatively high interest, and they had upside potential because they increase in price as the under-lying stock increases in price. John would either short the underlying stock (the sale of a security that the seller does not own, based on the belief that the seller will be able to buy it back at a lower price, thus profiting from the difference) or he would short call options (a derivative security that gives the holder the right but not the obligation to buy a specific amount of stock at a specific price during a specified period of time). If the stock price rose, he would give up the bonds and lock in profits. If the stock went down, the short position would provide downside exposure. If the stock did not move, John would collect the option premium or interest from the short stock position. In any scenario, the strategy involved receiv-ing interest from the bond.

Once John was able to show success with his strategy, he found it easy to bring in new clients. In 1977, he and a partner set up their own stock bro-kerage company, using convertibles as the mainstay of the business. Both partners invested money, John's share coming from a bigger mortgage on his house. "I had a very close-knit clientele that had a great deal of confidence in me. It was also the right thing to do for the clients," John says. "By focusing on the investment advisory business, I could really concentrate on two things—managing clients' money and providing top-notch service." A few years later, they received the attention of an institutional investor. After meeting with the client and showing off their impressive performance and investing discipline, they earned the business.

In the early eighties, John recruited his nephew Nick Calamos, who received an economics degree from Southern Illinois University and an MS in finance from Northern Illinois University. Nick started at the company as a computer programmer and built the computer systems and quantitative tools. "As soon as I saw my first personal computer, I knew we had to have one," John says, shaking his head in disbelief that he ever got along without one. "Nick joined me right out of college, and he just ran with it."

Besides computerizing historical data, portfolios, performance figures, and overall office functions, Nick built a quantitative model that helped analyze convertible securities and the underlying stocks. This proprietary research system monitors and scans the entire convertible market for the best available investment opportunities. "The convertible side is very analytical," John says. "Especially the option component of the convertible, which enables investors to convert into the stock, and the fair value, which prices the option component. This is necessary because you want to know if you are paying too much for that option or if you are getting a cheap price." John was one of the first in the business to use option price theory in evaluating convertible securities.

This system enabled them to better evaluate stocks, which are the basis of convertible securities; the Calamos managers still take a close look at both the stock and the bond component. "It's three times as much work," John says of convertible-bond analysis, referring to the process of analyzing the underlying equity, the convertible features, and the credit analysis of the bond. While the manager rarely converts the bonds into stock, the bond's value is tied to the stock. That's because the convertible's value rises with the underlying stock.

Over time, the team noticed a plethora of companies—which looked attractive from an investing standpoint—that had stock, but didn't issue convertible securities. John and Nick stress tested a model of a portfolio of stocks, without investing in convertibles. After all, since the model was really looking at the underlying company, the model should work for equity investments. "You can't be a solid convertible manager without looking at the equity of the company," John says.

The models worked, so they took the test one step further by funding a portfolio with their own money. "I wouldn't invest other people's money unless I was first willing to invest," John says. The fund was a success, spotting growth companies that met their criteria; over time, the stocks handily outperformed the indexes. Thus, in 1990 the Calamos Growth Fund was born. "Our intention with the Growth Fund is to achieve long-term capital appreciation through direct equity participation in companies where the earnings growth and value are not yet reflected in their stock prices," John explains. Additionally, the Calamos Growth Fund planted the seeds for a mid-cap growth program that is now offered to separately managed accounts as well as institutional clients.

Understanding why the Calamos Growth Fund is categorized as a mid-cap fund is a lesson in convertibles. And who is better to discuss convertibles than John, who has written leading books on the subject, titled *Convertible Securities: The Latest Instruments, Portfolio Strategies, and Valuation Analysis* (New York: McGraw-Hill, 1998) and *Investing in Convertible Securities: Your Complete Guide to the Risks and Rewards* (Longman Financial Service, 1988). "The convertible bond market is really about access to capital," John begins. "Companies need access to capital to grow their businesses, and the companies that typically need access to capital are mid-caps. Mid-cap companies claim the sweet spot in the capitalization spectrum. Mid-caps are more likely to outpace the largest companies in the rate of growth, yet they may offer greater maturity and stability than their smaller counterparts.

"A large-cap company, such as GE, has billions of dollars in cash. Microsoft has billions of dollars. These large caps don't need access to capital.

They generate capital. If they need money, they can issue bonds and pay relatively low interest rates. "Mid-cap companies tend to be the real engines of growth in the U.S.," John says of the Growth Fund, whose median cap size is currently about $1.5 billion. "This gives us a solidly mid-cap complexion."

"Mid-caps are the ones creating jobs and ideas," John continues. "They tend to be the real innovators. At one point, Microsoft was a small-cap, then a mid-cap, and then of course a large-cap. The problem with this category is that it requires active management because they tend to become either big winners or big losers, what we call the creative phase and the destructive phase. Of course we focus on the winners—but they, too, are vulnerable to fall because they either get fully priced or they just lose momentum and their stock falls. For this reason, we don't advocate a buy-and-hold strategy. Yesterday's winner may be today's loser. Some investors think they can find some great stocks and hold them forever. However, we characterize ourselves as nimble, keeping the portfolios fresh and vibrant. This is why our well-defined sell strategy is as important as the buy guidelines. We have a very active strategy."

A Nimble Strategy

John mentions Lucent Technologies when explaining why the buy-and-hold strategy doesn't work: "Up until 1999, Lucent stock was a 'darling.' When it was trading around $70 a share, many investors considered it a relatively sound growth stock. In 2000, as the stock began falling, many investors held on, hoping the company's woes would turn around. Lucent fell to under a dollar a share after several quarters of missing Wall Street expectations and announcing multibillion-dollar restructuring charges." John adds that active management and managing risk are key components in his fund's strong performance.

In the world of mutual funds, active management translates into a turnover ratio, or the number of times the average stock in a fund was bought and sold over the course of a year. The fund's turnover, around

150 percent, is higher than that of the average fund in the mid-cap category, but in the case of the Calamos Growth Fund, it also reflects the
lower volatility—or risk— in the portfolio, which typically has 65 to 80
different stocks.

When considering risk, John says, "The best way to create wealth is to
manage risk." He accomplishes this through diversification among stocks
and industries, and he stays clear of companies whose balance sheets do
not meet his standards. "We're always measuring risk." As an added safe-
guard, the computer systems are programmed to constantly measure risk.

For example, in the fall of 1999, the Calamos computers issued a warning signal, indicating that technology stocks were overpriced. While the
managers took the system very seriously, they have found that it is often
early; so they remained in technology stocks a couple more months. At the
end of 1999, they decided to lower their risk exposure to technology
stocks and sold half their positions by March of the following year. This incredible timing saved their investors from an ominous freefall in technology stocks. Then to add to their fortunate timing, they diversified the
technology proceeds into healthcare, consumer-products, energy, and financial stocks. These stocks, the managers felt, would provide lower risk
and acceptable upside potential. "We shifted to a conservatively different
portfolio," he says.

"We designed an actively managed investment strategy so we could remain nimble, moving in and out of stocks, seeking to take advantage of
market changes," John states. In 1999, the Calamos Growth Fund was up
77.7 percent, and an impressive 26.6 percent in 2000, beating its Morningstar peer group of mid-cap growth funds by a full 17.4 and 31.2 percentage points, respectively.

The Research Process

When seeking new ideas, John utilizes a top-down, macro approach, always looking for themes. His views are secular in nature versus a short-
term outlook; when contemplating new themes, his time horizon is five

years. "We look at macroeconomic factors and long-term demographic trends in order to identify some attractive segments of the market. Our models help us explain the world," he says simply, "whether it's economic models or financial models. Our approach is based on our 30 years' experience and our sophisticated quantitative models. The computers will analyze data, but our experience dictates the direction, which is the dynamics of the political environment, our economy, and the world because history doesn't always repeat." In other words, the team chooses which models work better in which environment, and the 25-person software development team ensures that the portfolio managers and analysts are using the best tools possible. "We've had to shift very often with the changing dynamics of economics and the world. We are very cognizant of this.

"We are in a productivity growth environment," he adds, referring to the current long-term theme they are observing. "The gain in our economy is coming from productivity growth, which is a consequence of the rapid technology spending we've witnessed over the years. This is a productivity advantage that is evident in the United States and, ultimately, the world."

John points out another trend: increased global competition. "This will keep global inflation levels low," he says. "This global low-inflationary economic environment means companies aren't going to be able to easily raise prices, and margins are going to be thin. So we'll have no participation in the basic industries sector, but we will look at companies that will make other companies more efficient.

"Additionally, we feel consumer spending will continue." He points to H&R Block, the tax-preparation company, as a long-term holding for the fund. "H&R Block continues to show strong earnings growth, even amidst an economic slowdown." The Calamos team is forecasting strong earnings momentum.

Once the research department pinpoints attractive sectors, they seek the companies that are best positioned for growth. The quantitative model regularly rates 4,000 stocks on growth prospects, earnings potential and momentum, cash-flow return on capital, expected return, and private market and relative valuations. Additionally, the team's credit analysis for the convertible securities translates into identifying market inefficiencies. Calamos uses Moody's and Standard & Poor's bond ratings as a first step, but Calamos conducts its own continuous analysis because they crave the timely credit analysis; a lag in an analysis could lead to errors.

"The next step includes analyzing the equity," John explains. "We focus on what we view as the main value driver in the equity market—growth. We also use a cash-flow-return-on-capital evaluation procedure to more accurately estimate intrinsic value."

The system places those companies at the top that are likely to produce the highest long-term growth rates; stocks are eliminated if they don't meet the growth expectations that prompted their purchase. "This means rapid growth in regards to revenue, earnings, and expanding operating margins. Everything is analyzed on a relative basis," he says. "Back in 1998 we were looking for top-line growth companies in excess of 70 percent. Today, we're looking at 20 percent due to changes in the world."

At this point, the team unites the quantitative—both historical data and future projections—and qualitative research to consider potential catalysts for price movement. "While the quantitative models are vital to our process, the numbers in isolation do not make the decisions. These data simply give us the information to make better decisions. We believe the best prospects for success in volatile markets depend on knowledge and discipline. The result tends to be an approach unconventional in technique and highly competitive in performance. "Once we compile a list of companies in each sector that appear attractive, we study each company's business model and dig to see what's driving growth," John says. "We value the business based on free cash flows and the sustainability of those cash flows."

Once a stock is found, the team determines its suitability for the fund portfolio. This means reviewing the risk/reward parameters and the macroeconomic factors and assessing their impact on the portfolio's industry group and economic sector design. "Knowledge and discipline are critical to our investing methodology," John explains. "Managing money is both an art and a science. The model building is the science, and which models are appropriate for the current market environment is the art."

In December 1998, Emulex, a data-storage equipment maker, emerged on the team's radar. "Everything was in place," John remembers. "It was the right sector, and the fundamentals looked great—accelerated earnings, cash flow, and so forth." John bought the stock at a split-adjusted price of about 50 cents. "The stock continued to rank favorably in our models, and the stock started taking off." Over a year later, as the stock started approaching $80 a share, the Calamos team recognized that at the current price the company would have to deliver earnings growth of around 30 percent *forever*. The team sold a portion of the position, and the stock slipped in price. Suddenly, it took off again, soon reaching $100 a share. That is when the team sold the remaining shares, realizing a gain of 1,940 percent.

"Some of our models tell us earnings are growing for particular companies, and these companies are ranked among the 4,000 companies we review for earnings growth. As business cycles mature, earnings growth may continue, but top-line growth, or revenue, may falter. This is a signal to us that earnings growth is not going to be very sustainable."

Another success story was the purchase of chipmaker PMC-Sierra, which the team bought in February 1999 for around $19 a share, and sold in March 2000 for over $200 a share. "These were nice long-term gains," he says. As of this writing, shares of Emulex and PMC-Sierra are each about $11 a share.

The Sell Discipline

"We're very cognizant of realizing the long-term taxable gain status," John explains, "always seeking to be tax efficient. Every time we come to a 12-month holding period, we determine whether we want to continue holding the position." If the team is prepared to sell a stock anyway, the decision to eliminate the position is simple. However, if the team wants to continue holding the stock, they will sell the position, then buy it back 30 days later to avoid a 30-day wash sale. This IRS rule states that losses on a stock sale may not be used against gains if the stock is purchased 30 days or less before or after the stock sale. In big years, such as 1999 when the fund posted a 78 percent gain, just about all the gains were long-term gains.

Several other factors are more important than tax considerations. John will sell a company's stock under three scenarios: when the fundamentals deteriorate; when a more promising opportunity arises; "or when we determine that a company no longer has any additional upside on an earnings growth basis." John will add to holdings "when we realize detailed positive information on a company's financials. Conversely, we trim holdings or sell the entire position when we feel bad news transforms our positive outlook."

When a position is sold, the team does not allocate the proceeds to cash. "We have found this to be very dangerous; it's sort of like short-term stock picking, which we don't pursue for this fund. Allocating to cash when we're still constructively long-term bullish on the market can be very dangerous, because anything can happen over the short term. For example, say the Fed surprises the market by lowering short-term rates by 25 basis points. If you're sitting on cash, it's too late to get back in to take advantage of the news. This is how individual investors get whipsawed—by getting in when good news is released, then selling when bad news appears."

An Advocate for Investors

When John stops to consider the 100,000 or so individual accounts and shareholders who are entrusting his organization with around $11.7 billion, he often thinks back to the account he managed for his parents. "Part of my job as CEO is to be the client advocate," he says firmly. "When talking to my company, I speak for the client. If I make a promise to a client, it is going to be kept. We always put our best foot forward."

John keeps a close eye on customer feedback. "It's a great feeling when we receive strong reporting marks from our investors. It's an even better feeling when clients approach me." Obviously Calamos Asset Management is doing something right: The company was 2001's fastest-growing mutual fund company for the year.

But success means more than simply numbers to John. "It gives me great satisfaction knowing that I can help to fulfill individuals' dreams," he begins. "It's especially pleasing to know that our investment philosophy is in sync with the investor. It's very important that investors understand our investing process, which is really a significant portion of a long-term business plan that every investor has when pursuing financial goals." Indeed, when the Calamos team considers success, they think about their investors reaching their goals. "We don't keep a close eye on performance; we just stick to our investing process and discipline, and service clients."

One day a factory worker visited John's office. Calamos had been managing the company's pension fund for over 10 years. The man was getting ready for retirement and wanted to personally thank the Calamos team for their excellent performance. "He came in to thank us, and we spent a lot of time with him," John says, smiling. "We showed him around the office and introduced him to everyone that was available—he enjoyed shaking everybody's hand. It's important that everyone saw him because it's a good feeling to associate a face with what we're trying to accomplish."

John then grows serious, and says: "Whether it's factory workers, institutions, or individuals on the other side of the planet, I like to treat them all as if it were my parents' account."

CHAPTER SIX

WALLACE R. WEITZ

WEITZ
PARTNERS
VALUE FUND

❜ ❜ ❜

*W*ally Weitz knows how to build a successful investment company. But it is not what he has accomplished that makes his story so interesting, it is how he has done it. Since 1983, Wally Weitz has been consistently providing high-quality investment management at a reasonable price, and has built a loyal following along the way. He has also built an enviable track record; over the 10-year period through 2003 the Weitz Partners Value Fund ranked as one of the best in the mid-cap value category, returning 15.32 percent, a full 4.26 percentage points better than the S&P 500. *Winner's Circle* research ranks the fund number one in terms of risk-adjusted returns.

Solid performance has been key to his success. In 2000, a year that saw the broader averages decline sharply, Weitz Partners Value Fund outperformed its benchmark, the Standard & Poor's 500 Composite Index, by 30 percentage points by posting a 21.1 percent gain. Although the fund lost 0.9 percent in 2002, it still did far better than the S&P 500, which lost −8.3 percent.

Although much of Wally's success as a money manager can be directly attributed to his time-tested value investment approach, his childhood and adolescent experiences have certainly played important roles in virtually everything he has accomplished in his professional life.

Born in the Big Easy

Wally Weitz grew up in New Orleans. His parents divorced when he was only two. He was reared by his mother, a social worker, who spent time working for the Travelers' Aid Society, an organization that serves individuals and families in crisis due to homelessness, mobility, or other disruptive circumstances.

From there, she spent time at Tulane Medical School as a caseworker. Her primary responsibility was to help families and patients at the Charity Hospital, a practicing area for students. She also taught a class she called, "Trying to Turn Medical Students into Human Beings."

Wally's desire to work hard was quite evident during his youth; always working, he mowed lawns and washed cars. While staying with his grandparents in New Jersey one summer when he was around nine years old, he ran a small but successful retail business from their front yard.

"My grandparents had a big old house with a backyard full of raspberry bushes," he recalls. "I had to pick a certain amount of berries each day so that we could make jam and deserts, but my grandparents told me that I could sell whatever I picked above my quota from a little stand out front.

"It was a little embarrassing for my grandmother," he continues. "My grandfather was the small-town doctor. But I loved it and became very competitive. Every now and then I would call the local grocery store to see what they were charging for raspberries and would adjust my price up or down accordingly."

This was not the only time Wally showed a lot of creativity in business as a youngster. When he was sick with the chicken pox, someone gave him a loom, which he used to make potholders. Within a few days, he discovered that he could make a lot of them in a relatively short period of time. "I began to wonder if I could turn this exercise into another business opportunity," he remembers thinking. Not knowing which potholders would sell or for how much, Wally made large ones and small ones as well as washable ones and nonwashable ones. When Wally recovered from his sickness, he called a few friends and convinced them to sell the potholders door-to-door in the neighborhood. "After a little experimenting, I decided on a price that I would need to keep making them and remain profitable," he says. "I offered the potholders to my friends at this price, and they marked up the potholders as they saw fit. The system worked, and everyone was making money."

When Wally reflects on his numerous business accomplishments as a youngster, he does not recall any specific experiences in his mother's household that might have encouraged or motivated him to become so business-minded at such a relatively young age. "There was no sense of depravation or anything like that," he offers. "It was a relatively simple life, fairly comfortable and serene. And although we didn't live in the best area of the community, I wasn't struggling with any social stigmas. In other words, I didn't feel a pull to make money so that I could get out of the neighborhood."

In fact, the only conversation regarding financial matters that Wally remembers having with his mother concerned local television advertisements featuring small loan companies. They promoted seemingly low interest rates to attract prospective customers. "My mother would rant about how these companies exploited poor people, because they were promoting *monthly* rates," he remembers quite vividly. He pauses, then laughs. "In retrospect, that was my first exposure to "compound interest."

In 1961, when Wally was about 11 years old, his grandparents gave his mother $25,000. While $25,000 is a generous gift by virtually any measure today, it was particularly substantial back then because it totaled approximately five times his mother's annual salary. Realizing how important this money was to his mother, Wally's grandparents offered to introduce her to their stockbroker in New York City. "His name was Victor Miller," Wally recalls. "Meeting him was a very memorable experience for me. He took us for a big lunch, at which she was bored, but I was intrigued. On the way home, my mother and I stopped at a bookstore to purchase a book on investing in stocks. The book was *How to Buy Stocks*, by Louis Engle (Boston: Little, Brown & Company, now in its 8th edition, published in 1994). I enjoyed the book so much that I wanted to invest in stocks right away, so I started writing to Mr. Miller at his firm to ask him questions about investing, and he took the time to answer my letters and send information that helped me become more familiar with equities. Not long after that, I started investing."

Buying Stocks at an Early Age

Wally's first investment was 10 shares of General Telephone and Electronics. He bought it at $26 3/8 per share in September of 1961 and says he sold it at $42 per share in 1966. "I also enjoyed a steady stream of dividends along the way," he points out.

In May 1962, when President Kennedy had a showdown with the steel industry, the market dropped sharply. GTE fell from 26 to 19 in one day. The experience did not diminish Wally's desire to invest. Every time he would save a couple of hundred dollars, he would buy another stock. And with each investment experience, Wally discovered that he was either making money or learning another lesson that would eventually improve his abilities to select securities.

For example, when he tried to purchase shares in Comsat in the early 1960s after it was brought to market, he learned just how difficult it can be to make money buying initial public offerings. Another time, he tried to catch a ride on high-flying insurance stocks, only to discover the risk of buying stocks after they have already enjoyed a major move.

By the time Wally was in high school his interest in equities was so great that he was charting more than 100 stocks a day. When he entered college, he was still trying to identify a system that would work well for his investment needs, when he stumbled on a book outlining the investment insights of the legendary Benjamin Graham. "It was then that I began to discover value investing and how it can minimize market risk while building wealth over the long term," he recalls. "I didn't know it then, but the principles that I learned during those days became the foundation of all my investment decisions from that point forward."

Despite his tremendous interest in business, Wally chose to attend Carleton College, a small liberal arts college located in Northfield, Minnesota.

The decision was influenced by his academic parents (his mother also taught social work at Tulane and his father taught psychology at NYU), and he is now a strong proponent of the liberal arts approach to education. After he graduated with a major in economics, however, Wally could not deny his passion for investing. At first, he thought about joining a management training program at a large, well-established company, but after investigating several programs he decided that this career path would not be appropriate for him over time. "I figured that if I worked in this capacity at a large corporation, I would spend my career jumping from one division to another, getting transferred to different cities every few years and focusing on promotions, with little free time. In a nutshell, I felt my life would not be my own."

Wally saw the securities industry as a viable alternative because it offered him more flexibility, or as he puts it, "the opportunity to come and go as I pleased." He added: "My perception was that I could do a hard day's work and then shut the door behind me when I left until I returned the next day."

Ironically, Wally now looks back at his long history in the securities industry and admits that he wound up with a work life that he thought he wanted to avoid—long hours, and thinking about stocks, even during free time. However, he also says that if he could do it all over again, he would not change a thing. "It's all been by choice," he beams, "and I've loved it."

On to Wall Street

Wally was determined to work at one of the major securities firms. He obtained a list of the top companies and sent a letter to the first 12 on that list. However, when he noticed the name of the thirteenth company (GA Saxton, the firm for which Victor Miller had worked), he decided he would send that company a letter as well. "Mr. Miller had retired, and my family no longer had an account there. We had switched everything to a firm in New Orleans. But, as luck would have it, the operations manager offered me a summer job. When fall came, I had planned on going to busi-

ness school at New York University, but I was enjoying the experience at
G.A. Saxton so much, I decided to stay there and attended business school
classes at night."

But after just one semester, Wally dropped out. "It just wasn't for me,"
he says candidly. He remained at Saxton for two and a half years, which
he said was very educational and rewarding from a career development
standpoint. "I was the assistant to the analyst, Artie Dunn, who tracked the
500 stocks in which Saxton was an over-the-counter market maker," he
says. "He never mentioned Benjamin Graham, but he was intuitively a
value investor."

From there, Wally worked as a researcher for three stockbrokers who
were managing discretionary accounts for individuals and small institutional accounts. "One day the president called me in to his office and said,
'you are doing a fine job, and we're not paying you much so there's no
problem, but what would you like to do with your life?' I was only 22 at
the time, but I told him I would like to manage money like the guys I was
working for. And he said, 'that's great. Go get some [money].'

"My conversation with the president of the company got me to focus
on what I needed to do in order to manage money. I didn't want to constantly call people for business, like most stockbrokers. That idea terrified
me. But if I went to work for a firm that already had the assets, such as a
trust department or a mutual fund company, I would have no control over
the accounts."

When discussing the situation with his wife one day, the conversation
shifted from his job aspirations to where they would like to raise a family.
"We considered my hometown New Orleans, as well as Minnesota,
where we had gone to college. But we settled on Omaha, where she had
grown up."

Wally proceeded to contact prospective employers in Omaha and
landed a job as a broker with a small regional firm. "The salary wasn't
much," he remembers, "but the opportunity was excellent. Since the
firm had no training program, I had to learn virtually everything on
my own—from researching stocks to finding clients. I also had the

opportunity to focus on the type of business I wanted to grow. I eventually settled on high net worth investors who had the potential to give me discretionary accounts."

Initially, Wally targeted doctors in the area whose names he had gotten from the Yellow Pages. He landed a few clients who wound up giving him quality referrals. Influenced by his exposure to value investing, Wally found success by offering investors high-quality investments selling at relatively attractive prices. "For example, quite often I would buy 100 shares of Berkshire Hathaway, which back then (1976) was selling for around $300 a share. It didn't bother me that these were one-time trades. I was enjoying the process of helping people and building personal relationships. And my clients respected the approach I was taking with them."

Early on in his career as a stockbroker and long before it was fashionable, Wally knew that having a fee-based business was much better than trying to build a business based primarily on transactions. In fact, since many of his clients owned the same securities, he considered creating a money management subsidiary so he could pool the accounts. Another thing that Wally did back then that few brokers ever thought of doing was to keep track of each client's portfolio on a desktop computer. "I had all the information on a computer, which was very unusual for a broker in the seventies," he recalls. "I did that for ten years and gradually built up a following with all types of investors and eventually created a steady stream of referrals."

Wally couldn't figure out a way to create a money management subsidiary at his firm, so in 1983 he left to start his own. He was very fortunate to get a lot of support from the president of his firm before he left. "He basically let me set up the business right from my desk so by the time I launched my firm, I was ready to hit the ground running." With his wife's encouragement, Wally approached several clients who said they would follow him. When they did, he pooled their assets in private partnerships and charged a flat 1 percent on their assets, like most mutual funds.

It proved to be a good strategy, but success didn't come without a few struggles. For example, one of his biggest clients didn't invest as much money as Wally had hoped for. "When the client asked what's the minimum, I told him $50,000. He said, all right we'll put $50,000 in, but I had been counting on him to invest over one million." Fortunately, Wally received enough money from other clients that he was able to launch his firm with between $10 and $11 million in total assets. "Considering that our overhead was very modest, I felt that asset size gave me some breathing room at the outset."

When Wally started his business, he didn't charge a commission for the sale of any fund shares. It is a practice he has never changed, and he believes it has always proved beneficial. "Remaining a no-load fund has enabled us to provide maximum value to investors and remain close to our shareholders at all times," he says.

Wally says he has never given much thought to expansion for its own sake. For example, a number of high-profile companies expand operations as well as their distribution channels in an effort to increase assets. Wally has been satisfied, as the saying goes, to stick with his knitting. It may not have seemed like a good strategy when other fund companies were building out their businesses and bolstering their bottom line during the boom years of the late 1990s, but his strategy has helped insulate his company from market downturns. "I always kept focused on this business model during the bull market because I simply felt fortunate to manage other people's money," he says. "I feel like I get paid to do my hobby. Why would I ever want to do something that might jeopardize what suits me and the firm well and has been good for investors?"

A Value Approach to Investing

Wally employs a value-oriented investment approach, focusing mainly on well-managed, financially sound corporations with low price-to-earnings ratios relative to the broader market. Typically, these companies are not capital intensive and have solid prospects of experiencing an expansion of earnings over time.

In his search for investment candidates, Wally pays as much attention to the intangible values of a company as he does the measurable data. Although Wally remains true to his value style, he is not adverse to spending a little extra to own shares in a solid company with what he believes are superior characteristics.

The influences that made him become a value investor were evident early in his life. His family's first broker was a value investor. When he landed his first job at a small brokerage firm in Omaha, he was exposed to the work of Benjamin Graham, and he had access to his boss's close friend, legendary investor Warren Buffett. "I would send questions through my boss, up to Warren, but the questions were about *how* he invested, not *what* he was buying." As a result of all of these influences, Wally embraced the idea that when you invest in equities, you are buying a piece of a business, and successful investing over the long haul depends on your ability to identify the value in these businesses before most investors do.

Wally believes the best way to recognize value is through intensive bottom-up research. Although he uses what he calls old rules of thumb to pinpoint potential investments, such as eight times earnings for savings and loan stocks, 10 times earnings for commercial banks, and so on, he does not have a set formula for conducting his research. "After all of these years, I wish I could say that I follow a specific pattern," he admits, "but because every business is unique, as are the people who run these companies, it's impossible to develop a so-called system that will uniformly work in all market environments."

When Wally finds a company he likes, he tries to determine a realistic takeover price that an intelligent buyer might pay; a price investors might dole out when the company realizes its full growth potential; and a valuation investors would pay when not preoccupied with factors unrelated to the company, such as geopolitical events. After he buys a stock, Wally usually holds it long-term, averaging over five years, versus his average peer in the Morningstar mid-cap value category holding period of under one year. If the stock temporarily disappoints, he will reevaluate his reason for buying it, and if he believes the fundamentals remain relatively attractive, he will consider using the decline as an opportunity to purchase more shares and lower his average cost.

Wally typically focuses on mid-sized companies. The average market capitalization of stocks in his fund is currently around $6.5 billion. Occasionally he will venture into the micro-cap world, but rarely. For example, he currently has a position in Intellegent Systems, an $8.5 million market-cap company. "I know management well and I like them," he says. "The stock sells around a buck and a half, but I think it could go to $4 or $5. But this is not the typical micro-cap company selling at an attractive price. This one has promise. Many others selling at attractive prices are what I call 'permacheaps' because of their lackluster fundamentals."

Whether he is buying shares in a large company, small company, or somewhere in between, Wally says he takes the time to get to know the people and how they think. He says it is particularly important to become familiar with the management of small- and mid-sized companies because of the significant impact they have on earnings. Regardless of the size of a company, Wally feels the key to finding a good investment is to find the two or three key variables that will determine whether the business succeeds.

Wally says he doesn't have to find companies that are underresearched by the Wall Street community. He will focus on stocks that, he says, everyone else can see. "The stocks that prove to be winners," he adds, "are usually either too controversial, too boring, or require too much patience. But that's the sweet spot for us."

A Case Study

One stock that describes Wally's investment process as well as his success as an investor is Berkshire Hathaway, a holding company owning subsidiaries engaged in businesses as diverse as GEICO, General Re, apparel, building products, candy, and flight services. Berkshire Hathaway is run by Warren Buffett.

Wally bought the stock for the first time in the mid 1970s when it traded for about $300 per share (a share of Berkshire currently trades in the $90,000 range). "When I purchased the stock," Wally recalls, "Warren Buffett had been around for 20 years, but a lot of people had not yet heard of him. That's because his company was complicated for many people to understand given the fact that it was—and still is—a combination of many different public and privately held companies. From my perspective, however, the company was still simple enough or small enough that I could look at it piece by piece to determine its value. And when I did the calculation, I determined that the company was worth $400 or $500 per share at the time. To me, it was a classic value play."

Over the years, Wally says he has given away Berkshire shares from his personal stake to charitable organizations as part of his philanthropic pursuits. He has also enjoyed success trading shares in the company. In fact, one of his biggest mistakes in the business was selling some shares when they reached what he believed to be an overvalued price of $600 per share, hoping to buy them back at $400. "Unfortunately it only reached $425."

More recently, Wally has enjoyed success with interest-rate sensitive financials, specifically banks and thrifts. In the late 1990s, many quality companies were selling at historically attractive price-to-earnings ratios, among them Washington Mutual, Northfork Bank, Greenpoint Bank, Countrywide Credit, and Astoria, just to name a few. As their valuations continued to come under pressure when the Federal Reserve raised interest rates, Wally kept increasing his positions in these companies. Once interest rates started to fall in 2000 and consumers began increasing the amount of money that they borrow, their stock prices rose sharply higher. In what has been a difficult market for most managers, these holdings have proven to be major contributors to Wally's success.

Learning from Mistakes

Every manager—no matter how successful—makes mistakes, and Wally would be the first one to tell you he is no exception to the rule. The reason: He understands that making mistakes and learning from them are critical in the development of any successful investment professional.

"A recent mistake came in the late 1990s during the market bubble," he recalls. "I managed to steer clear of those areas that have since collapsed and may never come back, such as the dot-coms, but I overestimated the potential of some fundamentally sound companies whose values got pricey in this environment. For example, back then I saw cable modems as a subscription business with repeating cash flows and other good business characteristics, but I underestimated the impact that the dot-com bubble had in inflating the valuations of these companies. In effect, I got carried away with how much a cable subscriber was worth and ended up owning companies like Adelphia and Charter. When the proverbial music stopped and the lenders could no longer lend money to these companies for the purpose of building out their systems, the companies discovered they were highly overleveraged."

Wally says one of the most common mistakes people make when they invest is underestimating the seriousness of the hurdles that a company must overcome to enjoy sustained earnings and improving valuations. "Fully understanding the problems and their impact is sometimes more important than knowing when to buy," he says.

A Final Word

Through it all, Wally Weitz has learned lessons, made money for his investors, and enjoyed the ride every step of the way. As he looks out to the future, amid the current downturn, he still believes there is much to accomplish, but he says his driving force will continue to be the same. "We have a strong, deep organization now, but the goal is the same: We continue to strive to provide clients with high-quality investment management at a reasonable price; everything else should take care of itself."

CHAPTER SEVEN

RICHARD F. ASTER, JR.

MERIDIAN
VALUE
FUND

❯ ❯ ❯

*I*t is no wonder Rick Aster leads the pack in the mid-cap core category, according to *Winner's Circle* research. As many investing professionals rode the markets up in the late 1990s bubble only to collapse in the early 2000s, Rick stayed true to his disciplines, producing strong absolute and relative performance for the Meridian Value Fund he founded. Most striking about Rick's discipline and philosophy—and a true testament to his staying power—is his ability to perform in good markets and bad.

Even as Rick was cautiously managing the fund's assets during the peak of the bubble in 1999, taking far less risk than his counterparts, the fund still earned 38.3 percent, around 17 percentage points above both his peers in the Morningstar mid-cap core category and his benchmark index, the S&P 500. In 2000, the year the market started collapsing, the Meridian Value Fund gained 37.1 percent, while the index and his peers lost money that year; he outperformed the index and his peers by a whopping 27.69 and 46.2 percentage points, respectively. In 2001, the fund generated another double-digit percentage year for shareholders, rising 11.7 percent, while the average comparable fund produced negative results. Although the fund was down 13.36 percent in 2002, it still managed to outdistance comparable funds and the broader averages by a meaningful margin, while taking less risk than the average peer. From 1998 through 2003—a five-year period marked by a bull, bear, then bull market—his fund returned 19.84 percent versus only 0.77 percent for his peers, ranking him as a solid number one among other funds in the mid-cap blend category.

In recent years, the media have applauded Rick's accomplishments, and assets have been pouring into the fund. In the past two years alone, assets under management have soared 10-fold to more than $1.5 billion, with Rick always prepared with new ideas or adding to existing positions. Indeed, the fund did not escape the bear market unscathed, but while many fund managers have altered their strategy markedly during the current downturn, Rick sticks to his disciplines: buying shares of high-quality companies selling at favorable prices and positioning his shareholders for the long haul.

The Beginning

Rick Aster is certainly no stranger to the financial industry. He has been analyzing securities and/or managing money for more than 35 years. Born in Monrovia, California, his passion for investing began when he was a college student. He received both his bachelor's degree and MBA in economics from University of California in Santa Barbara, then became an analyst for the U.S. Treasury Department in 1968. Two years later he joined Newburger, Loeb & Co. as a special situations analyst in Los Angeles. In 1972 he joined Robertson, Coleman & Siebel (predecessor to Montgomery Securities, which was later acquired by Bank of America), a six-person investment research boutique at the time, in San Francisco where he was responsible for formulating the firm's economic overview and investment strategy. His primary areas of research included emerging growth stocks and special situations covering a broad number of industries. Rick impressed management and investors with his investing and market acumen, and was given further responsibilities: managing accounts on a discretionary basis.

With nearly a decade's worth of experience behind him, as well as credibility and a growing, solid track record, Rick was ready to be on his own and invest individuals' money full time. In 1977 he started Aster Investment Management in Larkspur, California, investing primarily in small- and medium-sized growth stocks. During his early years in business, Rick conducted exhaustive work trying to find the right growth companies at reasonable valuations.

By 1984 his success managing individuals' money prompted him to open his first mutual fund, a no-load fund called the Meridian Growth Fund. In this fund, Rick seeks fast growing small- and mid-cap companies, but at a reasonable price. With this approach, he has shown that he can provide superior returns, but without the high volatility usually associated with these stocks. Over the five years preceding November 11, 2003, which encompasses both the peaks in the markets of the late 1990s and the lows in 2003, Rick led this fund to a five-year return of 16.37 annualized return, over 16 percentage points better than the S&P 500.

In 1994, Rick formulated another investing philosophy. "I've always been a fundamental investor," he says. "Over the long-term, stocks will have a high correlation with earnings. If earnings are growing, stocks will follow. In my mind, there have been two ways to approach this investing. One is a growth strategy, looking for companies with $500 million to $1 billion in revenue, with the potential over a number of years to reach $5 billion. Investors will participate in this growth through the appreciation of the stock. The second approach is on the value side, seeking companies that are selling at reasonable valuations."

Rick then moves to the thesis of the newer philosophy. "After following the small-cap sector for so many years, it seemed there were plenty of companies that miss their earnings numbers for several quarters," he says. "Consequently, their valuations would fall dramatically—usually 50 percent or more for the ones we were looking at. Many recovered, getting their businesses back on a growth track. However, many of these stocks fell hard when they missed their earnings projections quarter after quarter because, one by one, the securities analysts following these firms would abandon them, putting intense pressure on their valuations."

Rick spent several months back-testing varying assumptions with historical data from 1982 through 1994. Specifically, he wanted to know how an investor would have performed had he or she bought shares in out-of-favor companies, predominantly small- and mid-cap growth stocks, soon after they announced an increase in earnings following four consecutive quarters of "year-over-year" earnings disappointments. The holding period would be between 12 months and 18 months. He noticed that over the years he studied, when companies developed problems and reported down earnings, it took a long time for them to fix the problems. "It never happened in just a quarter," he says. "Companies generally didn't really know what hit them for a while, and then it took a while to fix whatever the problem was. In the meantime, the stocks would decline substantially. However," he continues, "there were a lot of good companies I found that did fix the problems, with great investing potential if you could spot the right ones." The research validated that such a strategy would likely outperform the broader market over the time horizon studied.

"If we can buy the stocks of these companies as they approach the point where their earnings are about to rebound, their valuations should be reasonable in comparison to their multiples and the multiples of their industry peers," Rick says. "Furthermore, if you bought the stock at the point of the earnings turn, you would benefit not only from a resumption of earnings growth, but also from an expansion of the P/E multiple. "In general, my belief is that these stocks no longer had much downside risk because they had already fallen sharply in valuation, and they would begin to perform relatively well once the underlying companies started realizing a sustainable growth in earnings again," Rick notes. He was right.

Some observers might call Rick's strategy "contrarian" since he is effectively scooping up shares of downtrodden stocks at beaten-down prices. However, this description doesn't accurately reflect the ideology behind the investment approach. "When companies have pressures to achieve certain growth targets, they are bound to make mistakes that result in temporary earnings declines, sometimes for four consecutive quarters," he says. "So I think we are simply being very realistic about the nature of business in a volatile economic environment."

The fund was originated in February 1994, with around $500,000, approximately half of which was Rick's money. While Rick understood that past performance is no guarantee of future results, his research showed that such a strategy was likely to outperform the broader market over time. "The smaller the company," Rick observed, "the better it seemed to work, mainly because the small-cap segment of the market is much less efficient than the large-cap arena."

The Investment Process

The investment process behind the Meridian Value Fund is relatively straightforward:

Rick starts with a universe of 400 to 500 companies that have had three consecutive quarters of earnings declines. He narrows the list by focusing on factors such as companies' market positions, the growth rates of the markets in which the companies operate, the historic returns on capital generated by companies, and the strength of the balance sheet. Once he narrows his monitor list to a manageable number of investment candidates, Rick performs fundamental analysis to determine whether the underlying companies are good businesses to own. "We look at the problem areas of each business to determine if they can be solved or if they may be problematic longer term," he says. "We look closely at the amount of debt owed by companies in relation to cash flow generated. We also evaluate each company's competitive position. Generally, we want to focus on companies that are leaders in the markets in which they operate."

Rick evaluates a company's competitive position in several ways. He studies industry reports provided by sell-side analysts. He scrutinizes each company's financial reports, and talks to the managements of companies under investment consideration, as well as their competitors and suppliers, and he attends numerous conferences and listens to conference calls. "We don't have to travel too much to meet with management or attend conferences," he points out. "We usually contact companies by phone or meet management when they pass through San Francisco. As for conferences, many are held in the Bay area or are offered via a web cast."

Focusing on a stock when the underlying company is struggling through a period of down earnings may not seem like a prudent investment strategy, "but a stock is usually most attractively priced when its fundamentals appear questionable. If we wait until the fundamentals have clearly improved, the valuation has usually moved up because investors will have already priced the improved outlook into the security," Rick points out.

Once Rick identifies companies that do not have insurmountable problems, he tries to determine what they need to do to generate earnings growth again, and what the earnings potential is likely to be in a normal economic environment. From there, he identifies the price he is willing to pay for each company. When Rick feels the valuation of a company is attractive, or at least reasonable, and fundamentals are improving and can be sustained for a couple of years, he will often buy the stock. Various valuation metrics are employed, including price-to-earnings (P/E) potential (achievable within two to three years), and discounted free cash flow analysis. "In our discounted cash flow models, we use a cost of capital assumption of about 9.5 percent, and a terminal P/E multiple of 15 to 16," he says.

Rick says he tries to maintain a diversified portfolio and rarely, if ever, looks at index weightings and how a fund's composition by industry compares with a consultant-imposed benchmark. However, he is very much aware when one industry group is overrepresented or underrepresented in the portfolio. Currently, the Meridian Value Fund consists of 76 companies in 24 industry groups with a market capitalization of between $1 billion and $10 billion. "For the past year or so, the fund's median market capitalization has hovered in the $2 billion to $3 billion range," Rick says.

On average turnover is about 75 percent, holding a stock for just over 1.3 years. "Turnover tends to increase when the market is strong, because improving operating results tend to be recognized quickly," Rick notes. "However, in a weaker market environment, it often takes longer for a turnaround to develop, and longer for the market to recognize that turnaround." Rick will typically add to a position if he gains confidence in the company's ability to increase profit margins or revenue growth, and the valuation, in his judgment, remains attractive.

Since small companies can be illiquid and the fund tends to hold stocks long-term, Rick focuses primarily on companies that have what he calls an "acceptable level of trading volume." For most securities, that is usually around 200,000 shares a day. Rick says he will sell a stock if the valuation reaches his initial target price and the underlying company's fundamentals have either stopped improving or are deteriorating again. He will also unload a security if the valuation becomes too lofty, in his estimation, regardless of the company's fundamentals. "If we lose confidence in a company's ability to turn its operating results around, and doubt our investment thesis will come to fruition, then we will also sell the stock and move on," Rick says.

Case Study

A good example of a stock that has met Rick's strict investment criteria and ultimately proved to be a sound investment for shareholders is Omnicare, the largest provider of pharmaceuticals to nursing homes and assisted living centers and the fifth-largest contract research organization.

"Omnicare distinguishes its drug distribution operation through its geriatrics-specific formularies," according to Rick. "In effect, the company ranks drugs based on their clinical effectiveness and cost, and then recommends to its customers which drugs they should buy." From the second quarter of 1999 until the second quarter of 2000, Omnicare had five down quarters. After hitting a high of $41 in 1998, its stock fell as low as $7 in late 1999. The fund established a large position in the stock between March and June 2000. Average cost: $10 or $11 per share.

In the late 1990s, Omnicare faced a problem that put a severe damper on revenues, "but not due to management or its overriding business model," Rick says. "Revenues came under pressure due to legislation passed by the federal government. In an effort to control escalating health care costs, the Balance Budget Amendment of 1977 reduced nursing home reimbursements, which negatively affected revenues at nursing homes across the country. In turn, nursing homes asked suppliers to rene-gotiate their contracts. Against this backdrop, Omnicare's revenues de-clined faster than the company was able to adjust its cost structure to the new environment.

"In 1999 and 2000, Omnicare restructured its operations to cut costs. And the inflection point where the cost savings began to outweigh the revenue declines came in the third quarter of 2000, just about the time when it appeared the worst for the company was already behind it," Rick recalls. "When we stripped the company's short-term business problem from our analysis, we could see that Omnicare was a clear market leader with substantial market share, strong management, and a solid business model for the future. And although the company had a lot of debt, indicat-ing it had grown in large part through acquisitions, it also generated signif-icant amounts of free cash flow. Moreover, it was now using that cash flow to pay down debt rather than make further acquisitions."

At this point, Rick remembers, Omnicare had reached a trough in terms of its earnings decline. What's more, he believed the company had sufficient cash flow to support its debt even if the turnaround took longer than he anticipated. "On top of all this," he stresses, "the stock was rela-tively inexpensive." At the end of 2000, Rick expected Omnicare to earn approximately $1.15 in 2001 and at least $1.25 or more in 2002. "So, at $10 or $11 per share, the stock was trading at less than ten times the earn-ings that we thought would be realized in two years," he recalled.

"At that point, with the market valuations the way they were in 2000 and healthcare being relatively unaffected by the economy, we figured that it was quite possible that Omnicare might achieve a P/E multiple of 20 if it achieved a full turnaround. Our thinking was that if we bought at its then-current price $10 or $11, we could easily see its stock price double within 18 to 24 months. But there was yet another thing that made this stock attractive.

"Omnicare operates in a market that is experiencing secular growth. At that point, we projected the institutional pharmacy market would grow 6

to 8 percent annually over time. Growth would be driven by 2 to 3 percent annual population growth as the population aged, 2 to 3 percent annual drug price inflation, and 1 to 2 percent growth from increased acuity
levels requiring higher drug utilization per patient. Since we expected
Omnicare to gain market share, company growth could be as high as 8 to
10 percent annually.

"In effect, we believed Omnicare had two sources of earnings leverage:
improving margins through cost reductions and significant revenue
growth. The company also had some other growth initiatives as part of its
game plan, but we viewed those initiatives as upside potential to the earnings that we were hoping would be realized."

Omnicare executed its plan. The industry grew as projected. Operating
margins have returned to normal levels. "The company is now, once again,
making acquisitions to consolidate the industry further," he says. "And
management is using the ever-increasing free cash flow that the company
generates from operations to keep its balance sheet in good shape, and pay
down debt that is used to finance the renewed acquisition program. Today,
Omnicare sells for about $45 per share, around four times our cost basis.
When we made our initial investment in the company, we owned about
$2.5 million worth of Omnicare stock. Today, thanks to the stock's appreci-
ation and the increase in assets in our portfolio, we own $44 million worth
of the company."

In early 2004, Rick viewed Omnicare as a viable security to own. "The
current P/E multiple, while getting high, is around 23.25. Business fundamentals remain strong, and we expect earnings to go from $1.50 per share
in 2003 to $1.95 in 2004. Of course, our outlook is not without some
concern. The reimbursement environment for the health care industry is
coming under pressure once again due to the fact that governments at all
levels are facing serious fiscal woes. As a result, it is quite possible that the
reimbursement environment could become less favorable than it has been
for the last three years. However, we think that the opportunities that the
company enjoys right now outweigh those risks and those risks are reflected in the valuation."

Learning from Mistakes

Like every portfolio manager, Rick has had his shares of miscues, but he has been quick to learn from them. Take his investment in Healthsouth Corp., a company that operates in-patient rehab hospitals as well as outpatient rehabilitation centers.

Like Omnicare, Healthsouth suffered four disappointing quarters due largely to the reimbursement changes that took place following the passage of the Balanced Budget Amendment in the late 1990s. "The company received pricing pressure from its customers and it took a while for management to adjust to it," recalls Rick.

But unlike Omnicare, Healthsouth was never able to generate free cash flow and had a lot of debt on the balance sheet. "Management gave compelling reasons for the company's lack of free cash flow and we believed them," Rick adds. "So we bought the stock about the same time we established our position in Omnicare, and held it for two years before selling. We probably would have sold it sooner, but it remained [in the portfolio] for as long as it did due to a lack of new ideas during that period."

Although Rick says he broke even on this investment, he now says he should have sold the stock sooner. "Even when the company started growing earnings, management was still unable to improve cash flow. And that is a red flag. But management's explanation was credible. We gave them the benefit of the doubt. The company, which had a history of related-party transactions, or so-called self-dealing, continued with these practices even during the turnaround process when we owned the stock. Management engaged in transactions that were disclosed in its 10-K, which were more for the benefit of the management team than for the shareholders. This fact, along with the lack of free cash flow growth, should have been clear signals to not be involved with this stock."

Managing Growth

Regardless of spectacular results, Rick still runs a no-nonsense operation at the time, with barely enough people to keep up with the work.

Consequently, expenses charged to investors are minimal. Even today, Rick jokes by saying, "We're always busy." The expense ratio for the Growth Fund today is a low 0.97 percent, 0.31 percentage points lower than his typical competitor.

The fund's success obviously has been well recognized: Assets under management are now over $1.5 billion, and growing. Can Rick handle the influx of new money? "We've been adding to some positions, and expanding across different-sized companies," he explains. Given the increase in assets over the years, and the ability to maintain solid returns, it does not appear Rick would have difficulties investing the money in solid ideas.

A Final Word

Through the good and bad, Rick Aster takes great pride in all that he has accomplished and what he has learned from his accomplishments and mistakes along the way. While his commitment to hard work, independent research, and sticking to his disciplines have played important roles in his success, he knows that he has had good fortune as well—even though he is still keeping expenses to a bare minimum.

As he looks ahead, Rick says he will take the same approach to his business life that he hopes investors will take to theirs when making investment decisions. "Always remember that past performance is no guarantee of future results," he says. "Just do the very best that you can do." It is a strategy that has served him—and his long-term investors—well.

PART III

, , ,

Small-Cap
Mutual Fund Managers

CHAPTER EIGHT

JEFF CARDON

WASATCH
SMALL CAP
GROWTH FUND

❯ ❯ ❯

J eff Cardon likes to brag, not about outperforming every other mutual fund in his category over three-, five-, and ten-year time horizons, and not about his firm's homey office, with views of the picturesque Wasatch Mountain. Besides enjoying conversations about his family, he likes to brag about his team, whose culture, he says, is one of the keys to his firm's success. "We've developed a culture here that is truly unique," he says proudly. "This is why we're successful."

Successful they are. Investing in the Wasatch Small Cap Growth Fund ten years ago through 2003 returned to investors 15.02 percent, over 7 percentage points better than the average small-cap growth fund, and almost 4 percentage points better than the S&P 500. Add to this less volatility and risk than the average small-cap growth fund.

Born in nearby Ogden in 1957, Jeff grew up learning the ins and outs of small business ownership. In fact, seeing his father manage his five-person title insurance company, Jeff recognized the impact of management ownership: "No one worked harder than my father," he says. "Then again, he had the most to lose." Interested in small businesses and entrepreneurial ventures, Jeff graduated University of Utah in 1980 with a finance degree. Soon after, he was hired by Wasatch founder Sam Stewart.

Sam, whose father was a stockbroker, founded Wasatch in 1975, after a career first as securities analyst at the Securities and Exchange Commission, then as a professor at Columbia University. Once he opened the doors to Wasatch, he continued to teach, this time at the University of

Utah, until Wasatch demanded his full attention. "I knew I wanted to be involved as an entrepreneur in a small company," Jeff says, thinking back to his father's days striving to build a business. "And I was also fascinated by the investing world. It seemed like an intriguing entrepreneurial experience, so I decided to join Sam's team.

"My resume is one line long," he says with a laugh more than two decades later. At the time, the three-person Wasatch group was managing individual accounts that totaled $8 million, a pittance compared with the nearly $7 billion in individual accounts, institutional money, and mutual funds the company now manages. The third member of the team was Sam's partner, a stockbroker who brought in his own assets to be managed. Jeff was earning $12,000 a year, and payroll was missed on a regular basis. Sam would visit the company once a week to check on progress. "I didn't even have a title, let alone a quote machine," Jeff says with a hint of astonishment. "I did whatever needed to be done to survive, and that included seeking stock ideas."

A few years later the early Wasatch group got its big break when Sam and Jeff earned two Salt Lake City–based institutional clients, together providing the money managers with around $40 million to invest. Jeff was pressed to find more companies that fit his criteria. In doing so, he sharpened his investment philosophy.

An Eclectic Philosophy

Eclectic is the word Jeff uses to define his early investment philosophy. "We were really trying to pursue companies that were undiscovered by Wall Street," he says, "though we had some companies in the portfolio that predated me, such as Pepsi." Within two years, as money was brought in and Jeff's investment philosophy was more finely tuned, "we were pretty much investing in undiscovered, growth-oriented small-caps that had potential for big earnings growth." Jeff feels that his interest in small-caps can be traced back to the days he watched his father build his small title company. "It made me realize that the owners of small-cap companies have everything at stake—with high inside ownership—and are endlessly devoted to making the company successful. Furthermore, some of these companies had tremendous upside growth potential that wouldn't be realistic for bigger companies."

In the early days, Jeff was relying on information from annual reports. With these data, he was analyzing companies' margins and balance sheets. As time went on and the team grew, the company gained access to information similar to what the big Wall Street firms used. With these additional resources, Jeff built sophisticated earnings models to understand what was driving the growth of the companies he was analyzing. By the time the operations were all computerized, with real-time fundamental and quote data, investing disciplines and investment processes were established.

A Team Approach

Today, the Wasatch team numbers 60, including call center individuals. Wasatch outsources functions that are not directly related to pursuing investment ideas or personal interaction with investors, such as shareholder accounting-related activities. Everything investing related is a team approach, even the ownership of the company. "We set up Wasatch just like the companies in which we like to invest," Jeff adds, "with high inside ownership." Wasatch instituted a stock buyback program in the early nineties. Stock is given to employees, and the program directs the firm to buy back stock from those who leave. In other words, the company is 100 percent owned by its employees, leaving no room for outside ownership. An additional benefit, Jeff says, is that they are not distracted by outside parties interested in buying the company. Jeff also believes that inside ownership helps to attract strong employees and provides a solid career path. Maybe that is why employee turnover is minuscule, and why no portfolio manager has left Wasatch since it started offering mutual funds in 1986.

Including Jeff, the lead manager of the Small Cap Growth Fund, there are 11 portfolio managers. Sam Stewart and J.B. Taylor are co-managers for the Core Growth Fund; Karey Barker and Ajay Krishnan are co-managers for the Global Science & Technology Fund and the Ultra Growth Fund; Robert Gardiner is the lead manager for the Micro Cap Fund; John Mazanec, Jim Larkins, and Sam Stewart are co-managers for the Small Cap Value Fund; Mike Gerding is the lead manager for the International Growth Fund; and Brian Bythrow and John Malooly are co-managers of the Micro Cap Value Fund. These managers are supported by a team of 12 analysts.

Intense due diligence is probably the best way to describe the Wasatch team approach to analyzing companies. Managers spend one or two days a week visiting companies that either are in their portfolio or are prospects for new investments. Newer analysts visit a minimum of 100 companies their first year. All told, over 500 companies are visited a year. When a manager visits a company, he or she is often accompanied by another team member. As each manager travels thousands of miles each year to obtain a firsthand look at prospective investments, companies are subjected to intensive analysis to ascertain their potential as rewarding investments.

When Karey Barker recently visited Pediatrix to investigate purported Medicaid fraud, she brought along Jeff. At the time, Jeff was not yet convinced that there was no wrongdoing. "When we're worried about a company, we find the most negative person on our team and take them with us," she says. After the team evaluated the executives' billing practices, Wasatch was satisfied that there was no wrongdoing. Thus assured, the managers quintupled their holdings to 2.5 million shares when the stock fell below $10 a share. Subsequently, the stock rebounded to the mid 30s.

"We come at them in waves," Sam says of the managers and 12 analysts who investigate a company before a manager makes a trade. "We have people probing and poking at a company in enough different ways so that we usually make good decisions." When visiting companies, the team will interview executives, employees, suppliers, and customers. Some of the questions they seek to answer include, Who is your number-one competitor? and Who in this segment gets the most respect from their peers?

"We believe that everybody has weaknesses in what they do, and the best way to compensate for that is to bring people in," Jeff adds. He equates their methodology to the Indian parable, "The Blind Men and the Elephant." In the tale, six blind men encounter an elephant for the first time. Each touches a different part of the elephant—from the tusks to the tail—and attempts to describe this complex object by studying its bits and pieces in isolation. Each blind man forms a completely different impression of the animal. But when all of them put this knowledge together, the truth emerges. "We believe that the more people who evaluate a situation and work together, the more it's going to look like an elephant," Jeff says. "It's all about relying on people you can count on to voice their opinion." In the end, it is the lead manager who makes the buy-or-sell decision.

Jeff refers to this getting-to-know-the-company process as "peeling the onion," the finding of truth as layers of the onion are peeled away, according to an old saying. "Essentially, we are going to know more about a company in a year than we do now," he says. "And a year after that, we'll know that much more about the company. The more we interact with either the company or its competitors or its suppliers, the more insight we get into who they really are; for the really great companies, we keep getting positive feedback." Jeff adds that he has even gained respect for companies that have stumbled. They earn his respect, he says, because of the way they handle the situation. "It's important to get to know a company through the good times and the bad times."

Because Wasatch focuses mostly on companies that aren't covered by Wall Street, or even the media, the managers rely not only on company inspections but also on assiduous research. This discipline provides the Wasatch team with a great deal of conviction when investing.

Growth at a Rational Price

While Jeff is commonly thought of as a bottom-up investor, one who first seeks companies, then considers industry trends and broader factors such as the economy, he actually doesn't look beyond the company. He sums up his investment philosophy this way: "We try to find America's best growth companies and stick with them."

He seeks companies with 20 to 30 percent annual growth, and prefers to buy them at prices he deems "rational." In fact, he likes to call himself a "growth-at-a-rational-price" investor. "We buy growing companies where we understand what drives their future profitability; then we can make good valuation judgments." This translates into PEG ratios, or price-earnings-to-growth ratios, of around 1. A typical company analysis includes studying financial statements, with an emphasis on increasing earnings per share, increasing operating margins, market-share growth potential, ability to maintain a competitive advantage, ability to perform consistently in various market environments, potential to take advantage of industry trends, and inside ownership of at least 10 percent.

The team develops an earnings model for every prospective or currently owned company. "We believe earnings growth is what drives stock prices, so we model these companies vis-à-vis their earnings per share. We pay attention to all the aspects of an earnings model, which are margin levels, margin trends, asset turnover ratios; this is essentially our DuPont model," a performance measurement method that helps consider the critical building blocks in return on assets and return on investments.

For every investment candidate, Jeff recaps the merits of the company and asks himself if the company is an ABGC, short for America's Best Growth Company. "This helps remind us what we are trying to do: Find great companies. Then we ask ourselves, is the valuation reasonable, or as we like to put it, rational?" In other words, can the team make money in the stock over a five-year time horizon? "It's a very simple exercise," he continues. "What do I think the earnings will be five years from now? What do I think the P/E ratio is going to be? Will the company have an unending ten-year growth horizon? Looking forward five years, I may give it a slightly higher P/E because I can say this is a high-headroom company, meaning that its growth rate could be high for a long time. It's pretty much a judgment call, but I do that for every company." Jeff maintains a spreadsheet that contains these figures.

"But at the end of the day, you've got to have some judgment," he says, then sums up the fundamental research process: "I am going to invest in companies for which I can make a credible case that the valuation is right." He leans forward in his chair and says with conviction: "This process isn't performed to find values. This process finds good companies."

Besides the numbers, of particular importance is the quality of the management. Jeff says that the longer he is in the business, the more he appreciates the quality of management and the company's culture. "The days of investing in simple businesses that can be run by anyone are over," he says. "Our economy has become too competitive. I don't think there's a business that will exist long term if it's run by a businessperson who isn't fully capable. The company that really has great management can do exceedingly well," says Jeff. "Look at General Electric. They built a company that's a leader in markets that don't strike you as being that thrilling." These types of companies have one commonality: "They're highly predictable companies that hold for the long term. These companies are attractive to us because we understand what drives their future profitability, and we can make sound valuation judgments." Jeff avoids cyclical companies because of their inconsistent profitability.

Jeff focuses primarily on four sectors: healthcare, technology, retail, and business services. Each company under consideration will have market capitalizations of under $1 billion when he first evaluates the company. Two of Wasatch's holdings are Orthodontic Centers of America and O'Reilly Automotive, an auto parts retailer. "We've owned O'Reilly stock since the early 1990s, and we've been buying more shares," he says. "We expect O'Reilly to realize a long-term earnings growth of 19 percent. The company has a P/E in the mid-teens, and it should report increased profits from a recent purchase of another 190 stores in Texas." Another holding is AmeriPath, an integrated physician group practice and laboratory management company providing anatomic pathology diagnostic services. With the population aging, Wasatch expects AmeriPath to grow 17 percent annually over the next few years. "We try to find America's best growth companies and stick with them," he says. These shares may be held for years.

Techne Corporation, another healthcare holding, develops and manufactures biotechnology products and hematology calibrators and controls.

Additionally, the company has a division that supplies information to the biotech industry, a service that will add to the company's long-term growth. "Their chief products are used in the research and development efforts at the end stage to assess the viability of potential new drug candidates," Jeff explains. "It's basically testing drugs with consumable agents. As opposed to a biotechnology company, whose stock could be up or down 50 percent due to an approval or disapproval from the FDA, this company relies on the biotech companies' research and development spending. So within a notoriously volatile industry, here's a company that relies on stable R&D spending—it's our backdoor play on biotech stocks." In the mid-1990s, Techne Corporation persistently appeared on Jeff's target list as a company to visit, emerging as a prime investing candidate in stock screening and DuPont models.

"Every time we went to Minneapolis on business, we would attempt to visit the CEO, but we never got our foot in the door," he says. He points out their 40 percent return on assets, and their 15 percent top-line and 20 percent bottom-line consistent growth. "It was one of those dream companies, but we wouldn't take the next step and invest without getting to know the company's management and culture." Finally, Jeff called the CEO's secretary to explain that his firm is a long-term investor and must meet the CEO prior to initiating a new position. "She called back and told me that the CEO would speak to me for an hour later that afternoon, and explained that he prefers to focus on business and stay out of public's view. He is a fabulous manager, she assured me; everybody in the company respects him, and Techne is a very well-run company. 'They just never went out and pushed the stock on Wall Street,' she said. We spoke to the CEO, then began buying the stock. Now, after owning the stock for seven years, we have a great long-run relationship with the CEO, and the performance has been terrific. He's become a good friend of ours.

"The reason we gravitate toward certain sectors of the market is because we spot growth opportunities. Technology is probably the fastest-growing sector, so we can't avoid it," Jeff explains, referring to more recent purchases in the sector. "During the dot-com bubble, we were underweighted in the technology sector because we just didn't understand how a lot of these companies would make money and how people were justifying valuations. And if we can't project earnings with a certain degree of comfort, which was often the case with many technology companies at that time, then we won't invest."

Still, even while he was avoiding the red-hot dot-coms in 1999, his fund gained 41 percent, part of which was due to holdings in profitable technology names. One technology stock he purchased, SDL, a chipmaker for the communications sector, was bought at around $3 a share in 1998. It was sold in mid-2000 for $110 a share, a rise of 3,560 percent (his fund was up 16.8 percent in 2000, almost 26 percentage points above the S&P 500 and nearly 21 percentage points above his average competitor). In a less-predictable sector such as technology, to limit the fund's downside exposure he may invest up to 1.5 percent of the fund's assets in a single company. "I just take smaller bets," he says, adding that he by far prefers a healthcare company with very stable numbers and a predictable story. "A technology company may be growing 50 percent and selling at a P/E of 20, but even though it may have a very high expected return, you have to recognize the associated risk of investing in industries subject to rapid change and intense competition."

Jeff places more money in the stocks that show the most risk-adjusted promise when he considers weightings within his portfolio. "I generally make my biggest bets in the companies that I understand the best and that have the most confidence that they are going to be bigger five years from now than they are today," he says. "This is in contrast to taking my biggest bets on the stocks with the highest expected returns."

In sectors such as healthcare, Jeff will invest as much as 5 percent of assets in a single company. One favorite, Amsurg, which acquires and operates practice-based ambulatory surgery centers, is presently just under 2 percent of assets. The stock is currently trading in the high 20s. Jeff bought the stock in 1998 for around $7 a share. "The stock really took off in 2000 in the aftermath of the bursting Internet bubble once investors started paying attention to good, profitable companies," he says.

Sell Discipline

When considering the sale of a stock position, Jeff takes into consideration a couple of factors. "One is, the company may get too big and the company just graduates from the small-cap growth category," he begins. "We are a small-cap growth manager. As an exception to the rule, we will ride some companies up into the $3, $4, and $5 billion market cap, but only if they have the growth rate to sustain that. The other factor is growth rates in a company may drop, not maintaining our discipline of 15 percent or higher." Jeff admits that the toughest sells occur when he buys a company based on its growth rates and later discovers that it does not meet his standards for high-quality management or that its growth rates are less desirable than he projected. "Of course, being part of a team that I can trust helps to safeguard against these kinds of risks," he says. "That's when our culture is particularly helpful: Every team member must voice their negative opinions."

Unlike many mutual fund managers who keep a close eye on risk measurements, such as beta, Jeff doesn't pay any attention. "If a stock is volatile that tells me I have an opportunity to buy it low. When analyzing a company, we are already considering risk," he says. "By constructing our financial models, we are considering risk by the fundamentals. If the fundamentals look risky, then we'll own less of the stock." When it comes time to place a trade, Jeff and team tend to be "somewhat contrary," he says. "We're not momentum players, chasing a stock when it's rising or selling a stock when it's falling. Because we tend to sell when the valuations get high, we're often selling when others are buying." The Wasatch Small Cap Growth Fund's turnover is currently around 40 percent, on the low side compared to its peers in the Morningstar category.

Secrets to Success

Jeff believes that the only secret to his team's success—besides a great culture—is using more commonsense than other investors. "When we create a portfolio, I conceptualize it more as a chessboard with moving pieces than a list of favorite stocks," he says. "When people try to figure out what the market is going to do that day or the next, that is a question that has nothing to do with creating a well thought-out portfolio. This has nothing to do with long-term investing. Investors with this line of thinking end up building short-term portfolios, which is probably what inflated the dot-com bubble. We try to see whether the emperor has clothes," he adds, referring to the Hans Christian Andersen parable. "We're really just a team of hard workers," he says, smiling. "And we love what we do."

CHAPTER NINE

JOEL C. TILLINGHAST

FIDELITY
LOW-PRICED
STOCK FUND

,,,

J oel Tillinghast has quietly built one of the mutual fund world's most enviable track records with a strategy that sounds categorically simple. Many wonder how he is able to successfully navigate a $26 billion fund in small-cap waters (his peers average around $500 million) that are for the most part illiquid. Yet, his low-trading, diversified approach has made the Fidelity Low-Priced Stock Fund one of the most tax-efficient, low-volatile funds among his competitors with a 10-year annualized gain of 16.03 percent and, remarkably, only two down years (down 0.08 percent in 1990 versus his Morningstar small-cap value category peers' average loss of 13 percent and down 6.18 percent in 2002 versus his peers' average loss of 21 percent—a year in which he was named domestic equity fund manager of the year by mutual fund tracking firm Morningstar). How is he able to consistently outperform his competitors and the indexes with minuscule risk? Experience is probably the best answer; in fact, Joel's experience began when he was only eight years old.

Joel has always been a whiz with numbers. Growing up in academic surroundings in Durham, New Hampshire, where his father was a biology professor and his mother was an accountant, he developed his mathematical talents early on. At a young age, he became fond of puzzles and any game that required the use of a calculator. Shortly after he turned eight, he came across copies of Value Line reports, to which his parents subscribed periodically. When looking at the reports, which offer fundamental information about stocks, his eight-year-old eyes saw a puzzle; he was always trying to figure out where the numbers came from, and where they were heading. "I enjoyed having a sea of numbers to look at, seeking progressions," he says.

His parents marveled at their young son's affinity for finance and investing. As the child continued to read the reports and listened avidly as his mother traded stocks over the telephone, they took his interest seriously and affably explained the investing process. And none too soon. When Joel turned 10, his interest moved to the next level: He made his first stock investments. He invested $100 in each of two stocks, utility-company Central Main Power and Beckman Instruments, a medical-products company. These two investments would later play a big role in his investment philosophy. He continued to trade, always placing $100 in each stock.

Joel graduated from Wesleyan University in 1980 and received an MBA from the Kellogg School of Management at Northwestern University in 1983. By that time he was certain that he wanted to combine his interest in writing with his long-time passion for investing. When he did not measure up in a speed-typing test for a newspaper-reporter position, he turned his sights on investing. "I never even had a chance to launch my career as a journalist," he jokes.

Ironically, his first job turned out to be with Value Line. He loved analyzing companies as an equity analyst and continued to successfully trade his account. Joel later realized that he belonged on the money-management side of the business. In 1986, he joined Fidelity as an analyst covering the industries of tobacco, coal, natural gas, personal care products, and appliances.

As a successful analyst, Joel relentlessly pitched Fidelity on new mutual-fund ideas. After passing on several proposals, Fidelity finally nibbled on one: a low-priced stock fund. The idea was to seek stocks selling below $15 a share, which, Joel felt, were a proxy for institutional neglect. Such stocks, he explains, tend to be mostly small companies that aren't well researched by Wall Street or big companies that are in a state of distress or turnaround. "Some of the bigger companies that fell into this category, for example, were Chrysler at $3 in the early eighties, then Citicorp at $9 in the early nineties," he says. "Where Wall Street and the big institutions saw neglect, we saw investment opportunities."

Fidelity back-tested the idea to see how it would have performed historically, then decided to test it with real money. Chairman Ned Johnson put $50,000 of his money into an account in which Joel helped make the stock selections according to his philosophy; six months later, it was outperforming its benchmark index, the Russell 2000. In December 1989, Fidelity launched the Fidelity Low-Priced Stock Fund. (Interestingly, one of two down years for Joel, –0.08 percent in 1990, was followed by his best year, up 46.26 percent in 1991.)

Joel expands on his philosophy: "Research about neglected stocks maintains that it's easier for a $5 stock to go to $10 than for a $50 stock to go to $100," he says. While many investors dream of ten-baggers, buying a stock for a dollar and seeing it rise 1,000 percent, stocks that are priced too low can be dangerous, even for Joel. "When you get below $5 a share, the stinkers outnumber the ten-baggers. In fact, if you bought all the stocks priced under ten, that wouldn't be a winning strategy," he said. "It's not easy picking low-priced stocks." Joel knows that stocks become cheaply priced for a reason; after all, a $3 stock is that price for a reason. In general, many investment professionals believe that stocks in the $5-to-$20 range need to be closely scrutinized prior to an investment. In some cases, the company is in an industry that Wall Street currently spurns or the company missed one or more earnings estimates. In other cases, the company's share price is headed far lower, or it is going out of business. This is where Joel shines. "You want to make sure you don't have complete wipe-out risk." Joel sums up: "This philosophy really capitalizes on Fidelity's strength—fundamental research."

The mutual fund manager has always been well supported by Fidelity's vast research. Joel is now supported by four full-time analysts that follow the companies in the portfolio and seek new ideas as well. Additionally, he has access to the remaining analysts, 90 in the United States and 166 worldwide, that are deployed along industry lines.

Mostly, Joel relies on the small-cap analysts to leverage his time. When he is pursuing new ideas, he says, if an analyst makes the case for an under-valued stock "and jumps up and down about it," he will take a closer look. For example, a few years ago, one analyst recommended shares of Sytner Group PLC, a high-end auto dealer in Britain. "Our analyst liked the company and said he would like to follow it." Joel initiated a position with a modest $90,000, with plans to add more shares later. Likewise, if an ana-lyst feels that it is time to sell a position—say a company in the portfolio has a doomed business model—Joel will further examine the company's situation and make the final decision.

Analysts also help Joel keep in close contact with the management of the companies that are in the portfolio, or prospective ones. On a given day, analysts will meet with as many as 10 companies at Fidelity's head-quarters, where Joel is located. "Out of ten companies that we see, there might be two that strike us as undervalued and have an attractive business model capable of producing growth for years to come," he says. "And there will be two companies that strike us as being overvalued or with a doomed business model, or both. Our analysts really add value by think-ing about the value of the business strategy. Additionally, the analysts con-stantly check in with companies, participating in conference calls and earnings announcements." To keep a close eye on portfolio holdings, or potential holdings, analysts will make in-person calls and telephone calls, visit company headquarters, and engage in other activities that may influ-ence an investing decision, such as visiting stores and plants, and even talking to customers.

The day prior to our interview, a Fidelity industry analyst discovered a small-cap temporary staffing company that was still unrealized by Wall Street. "Mainstream analysts often find that their most exciting opportuni-ties exist in the small-cap space," Joel says. In addition to his meeting with the temporary staffing company at noon, Joel's schedule for the day in-cluded meetings with a health-care company at 10 o'clock, a food com-pany at 11 o'clock, a construction materials company at 2 o'clock, and a health-care orthopedics company at 3 o'clock. Rather than attending all the never-ending meetings, Joel will typically participate "if the analyst is excited about the company, and says, 'This is your chance to hear the company.' All these meetings are essentially gated by the analyst."

Joel then points to the three-foot-high paper recycling bin and his computer and says, "Between the analysts, the overabundance of printed research I receive in the mail, and the plethora of e-mail sent to me daily, I try to keep up with everything."

Regarding the characteristics he pursues in a company, he admits his approach is nontraditional. "Although it seems completely logical to me, a lot of portfolio managers that seek undervalued companies don't compare a stock's price with value. This is my starting point."

In a bigger picture, he looks at his benchmark index, the Russell 2000. "What do I cut first? First I cut the companies that are unprofitable and have never been profitable—I will wait for them to become profitable before I invest in them." He concedes that he misses some winners this way, but he also misses the potential losers. "I also cut companies in which I believe management has difficult business issues relating to their business model. Next, I cut stocks that are visibly overvalued or where they have to work to get the value—value depends on how good the business is, how fast the business is growing, how volatile the business is. Lastly, I cut companies that are priced over $35 a share."

For Joel, a perfect company is one that can give its customers something proprietary that cannot be found anywhere else. It is also a company that is not in a commodity-like industry, with fierce competitors. Some of the questions he asks himself when evaluating a company include, Are suppliers in a position to easily raise prices and reduce profits? If the company raises prices too much, can the customers easily find a substitution? Are the employees in a position to raise their wages and eliminate profits? To illustrate this last example, he points to employees of securities firms' ability to jump to their competitors for better compensation.

To maintain his diversification, which he uses to undermine volatility, Joel keeps a close eye on industry-sector weightings. "If I become underweighted in a particular sector, I will either find surrogate companies that are closely related, or just loosen the criteria for the sectors by finding stocks that aren't as attractive fundamentally as they are in other sectors." He points to the technology sector as one that is difficult to pursue because "so many of the companies are unprofitable. As a result, I will focus on ones that were profitable at one time in the past, even if they are not currently profitable. The problem is, many of them just don't look real cheap to me." Because of this dilemma, his criteria for a technology stock are looser than his criteria for stock in other sectors.

When looking at a company's fundamentals, he considers items beyond the income statement. "I look at such items as pre–cash flow and a company's ability to fund growth internally instead of leveraging with debt." When looking at the balance sheet, Joel and team model the cash flow and create an earnings model; with this, he likes to keep earnings in perspective, with predictability three to five years into the future. "For some businesses, like technology, this approach would be crazy. A lot of technology companies have S-curves and even reverse S-curves," he says, referring to adoption rates. "It's crazy to try to predict where these companies are going.

For this reason, Joel analyzes different companies in differing ways. For steady-growth companies, he will look at the PEG ratio, which is used to determine a company's value while factoring in earnings growth and found by dividing a company's price-to-earnings ratio by the earnings-growth rate. He is interested in a PEG ratio of 1 or less. He looks at companies with earnings-per-share growth of 10 percent or better; "If it doesn't hit this level, then I'll look for something better." When scrutinizing the financials, he determines a company's liquidation worth by looking at its book value, or assets minus liabilities. "In general, the less debt the better, but it really depends on the industry." For example, he says, financial companies can support debt levels that would be perilous to industrial companies. Additionally, he compares a stock's earnings yield, or earnings divided by market price, to risk-free government bonds.

Asked to illustrate an analysis of a stock, Joel is quick to comply. In 2000, one of his analysts noted that homebuilders were trading at greatly discounted levels when compared to the value of their inventoried land. As home prices and land prices had been rising at that time, the analyst determined that the homebuilders' land and home prices were more than likely undervalued. D.R. Horton fit the right profile for Joel. At that point, because Joel had a position in Continental Homes, which was acquired in the late nineties, he had a position in D.R. Horton. "The year we bought D.R. Horton it earned $2.50, so it was trading at [a price-to-earnings multiple of] around four-and-a-half times earnings," he says. "The company had never had a down year in sales or earnings since it went public in 1992. Even though investors believe homebuilding is a cyclical industry D.R. Horton has had 23 years of up sales and net income, which has made it about as cyclical as General Electric." Joel bought the stock in the low-$10 range, when the stock had a book value—which he believed was understated—of $11½. (At the time of this writing, the stock is trading in the mid-twenties.)

As for all stocks that Joel selects for the Fidelity Low-Priced Stock Fund, he will sell a stock when the fundamentals deteriorate or when there is a decline in its competitive position. With a company like D.R. Horton, he would consider selling the stock if the company started behaving like a cyclical company, and profit margins began to contract.

In general, Joel prefers to continue holding a stock as long as the company is competitively situated versus its competitors. "In the case of D.R. Horton, its land-buying and capital allocations have been managed far better than those of its competitors." As of mid-2003, D.R. Horton was one of Joel's biggest holdings, comprising 1.5 percent of assets, or about $225 million.

Another reason to sell is when better value is found. "For example, if I'm holding a company and its earnings are growing 20 percent a year and selling at a P/E multiple of 25, and another company's earnings are also growing at a rate of 20 percent, but its P/E is only 12, then I will sell the expensive stock and buy the cheaper one."

Of course, another factor that may influence a sell decision is the fund's definition of *low-priced*, which was set at $15 or less at the fund's inception and increased to $35 in the late nineties. Joel says the increase came about primarily because he was forced to sell stocks at $15 that he believed had potential for far more appreciation. "We increased the price cutoff because we were selling our successes and keeping the dogs," he says with a sarcastic tone. The change also gives him more leeway to buy bigger companies that are considered turnaround plays. "Managing this fund is like growing tomatoes; you don't expect them all to germinate, but once one really takes off, it has the potential to cover for a lot of the others." Raising the price is especially helpful when managing a fund with such a large asset base.

Considering the enormous size of the fund, there is a lot to keep track of. With $26 billion in assets, around 50 times the assets of his average peer, Joel needs to manage differently than his peers. Small-cap funds generally keep asset levels to a minimum because size can be a hindrance; after all, small-cap companies are defined as those with market values less than $1 billion, with many having a value a fraction of that amount. Small-cap funds will close their doors to new investors (as Joel has decided to do five times through 2003), because it becomes troublesome finding new ways to deploy the money and too difficult to build or erase positions without radically moving stock prices and eroding returns. To illustrate Joel's conundrum, his fund is around nine times his average company's market capitalization (stock price times the number of shares outstanding), which is in the neighborhood of $3 billion (by comparison, the biggest companies, such as General Electric or Microsoft, have market capitalizations of over $300 billion). In fact, when he buys or sells stock in a small company with a market cap of $300 million, it can take six months to complete the transaction. The day prior to our interview, for example, his traders executed 128 trades for the day, purchasing stock worth around $100 million.

"We've had big inflows of money from investors this past year, and it can be challenging to put the money to work," he says. In fact, virtually the only way for Joel to buy up to 5 or 10 percent of a company in short order is if a significant event surges the trading volume to 20 times or more its average volume. As for smaller, less-liquid stocks, "Yesterday I placed an order to buy half a million shares of a company, but it only trades two million shares a day," he explains. "We only got 75,000 shares!" The most Joel can own of any company is 10 percent. If a company Joel is seeking has a market capitalization of $700 million, he could buy only $70 million at the most.

One reason he is able to manage an abundance of assets is his long-term investing horizon. With a turnover rate of only 23 percent, his average stock is being held around four years—good news for investors seeking high tax-efficiency. He is also aware of the high transaction costs, which can be bigger than the more liquid stocks "because of wide bid–ask spreads," he says. "I like to pick the winners and stick with them." He also holds around 950 small-cap stocks in the portfolio, far more than does his average peer.

Joel's biggest challenge, as many mutual-fund managers can relate, is fickleness among many investors. For example, as technology and Internet stock prices were skyrocketing in the late nineties, Joel remained disciplined to his investment philosophy, seeking only value instead of the high-flyers. To his dismay, he saw many investors redeem their Low-Priced Fund shares and buy into the mania. "I was just disappointed," he says, "but it's their money."

During that brief period, Joel underperformed other funds that were participating in the craze. In 1998, his fund posted a meager 0.5 percent return, underperforming the S&P 500 by 28 percentage points, then 5.1 percent in 1999, underperforming the index by 16.1 percent. In 1999 he received a letter from an investor who said, "I'm 54 years old and I won't be able to retire because of you." Joel says, "It doesn't take too many letters like that before you start feeling under the weather."

The biggest risk he took in 1999 was a small position in Intimate Brands, a division of Limited Corp. that operates Victoria's Secret. "The

most I adapted was by buying a highly profitable company that was building an Internet presence as an additional channel," he says. "It seemed like
an interesting Internet business, especially considering the huge amount of
traffic they were getting. Unfortunately, the traffic was mostly male non-
purchasers."

Before the craze hit the markets, Joel recognized the value of technology and was accumulating shares of Affiliated Computer in the
mid-nineties. The company offers comprehensive business-process outsourcing and information technology outsourcing solutions, as well as
system integration services, to both commercial and federal government
clients. "The company was attractive to me because of its solid long-
term contracts, with high visibility for earnings growth into the future,"
he says. "When we started buying the stock, it was selling for about 15
times the current year's earnings, but more interestingly, since earnings
were growing at a clip of 25 percent a year, its forward price-to-earnings multiple was extremely low. To our delight, earnings have been
growing faster than expected." Joel started buying the stock when it was
around $5 a share.

Joel believes the downside for a company like Affiliated has been
minimal because its long-term contracts have made the company more
predictable. "It's always been a possibility the company could stop growing, but the pipeline of already signed long-term contracts has provided
the company some degree of stability." Now, with the company selling
in the mid $50s, and the stock becoming pricey to Joel, he has contin-
ued to hold the stock because the company's growth has been far more
solid than that of other companies in the technology sector, such as
software companies.

Another example of a technology company that has been in the portfolio is Zebra Technologies. Joel bought shares in the company because
he was impressed with the company's products. "They have been the
leading bar code printer, and they have continuously added new features,
such as wireless bar code printers that have allowed people to better

manage inventories," he says. "If you ask a technology guru about the most exciting technology trends of 2004, I don't think they are going to say bar code printers. But then again, they have had big customers that have relied on them, such as Wal-Mart."

These days, investors are thrilled with his performance and, in particular, are happy that he sticks with his philosophy. Those who hung in there with Joel through the technology craze were treated to stellar returns, not to mention their avoiding potentially massive losses. In 2000, the Fidelity Low-Priced Stock Fund returned 18.8 percent, beating the S&P 500 by 27.9 percentage points. While investment professionals are always touting the necessity of discipline when executing a proven investment approach, few managers are able to repudiate the urge to deviate from their plan and join the latest trend or hot stocks. Joel is a testament to sticking to a proven investment approach, even when it falls out of favor among investors.

During another turbulent time in the markets, namely the financial markets' extreme volatility after the tragedies of September 11, Joel again proved that it pays to keep faith in a reliable, disciplined mutual fund manager. Though many of his holdings plummeted in price, particularly airline stocks, he carefully spent his time looking for value. With no shortage of undervalued stocks in the market, he managed to whittle down his cash position from around 19 percent to about 14 percent.

In 2001, he rewarded investors with a 26.7 percent return compared to a loss in the S&P 500 of 11.9 percent. The Fidelity Low-Priced Stock Fund was the best performing of 40 U.S. stock funds with $10 billion or more in assets, according to Morningstar Inc. Not surprisingly, investors couldn't send money fast enough to invest in Joel's fund, with about $3.5 billion in new money for 2001. Joel just hopes that investors will choose to stay with him for the long term.

Given this remarkable discipline and a winning investment philosophy, what has been the biggest lesson he has learned? A lesson he learned when he was 10 years old; the $100 of Beckman shares he bought back then is now worth around $14,000. The $100 he invested in Central Maine Power grew about 6 percent a year, around the dividend yield (he sold the utility a couple of years ago, but still holds Beckman Instrument). "It convinced me that you don't make the most money with 'yield' stocks," he says. Not surprisingly, recently his portfolio held about 8 percent of health-care stocks. Utility stocks? Zero percent.

CHAPTER TEN

BILL RICKS AND TEAM

AXA
ROSENBERG
U.S. SMALL CAP

▸ ▸ ▸

*T*hrough the years, AXA Rosenberg has gained wide acclaim, and a reputation for delivering solid performance for its investors across sectors with both its domestic and international equity strategies. In fact, Winner's Circle research ranks the AXA Rosenberg Small Cap fund at the top of its peers, with consistently strong long-term risk-adjusted performance (in the volatile five-year period through 2003 the fund returned 12.22 percent versus only 1.05 for the Morningstar category of all small-cap core funds). Importantly, it has done so by maintaining what it calls "intellectual purity" in every facet of its exhaustive research and money management process. Indeed, although many companies talk about their dedication to quality research and money management, few have demonstrated a deeper commitment to delivering the highest standard of quality than AXA Rosenberg.

A quantitative approach has served the company well: "When you are truly focused on maintaining a high standard of quality," says Stephen Dean, director of the firm's global product strategy department, "you are able to produce a result that is far more sustainable compared to an organization that is interested in pursuing the quick profit based on the latest fad." So the key decision makers at AXA Rosenberg simply enhance or refine their tried-and-true approach. Their investment principles are based on a belief that markets are not perfectly efficient at assigning a correct value to a stock, nor at identifying which companies will generate superior earnings in the future. AXA Rosenberg uses technology to rigorously examine the fundamentals and other price-influencing information of some 17,500 stocks worldwide, a task that would be almost impossible to perform by even an army of human analysts in a consistent manner. Then the manager builds a portfolio that contains the best combination of undervalued stocks that will add the most value while minimizing the deviation from the benchmark characteristics.

"At the risk of sounding somewhat philosophical," says Bill Ricks, chief investment officer and chief executive officer for North America, "we are constantly searching for that which is meaningful and unique in everything that we do. 'Ordinary' is not a word that would ever be used to define our organization."

Based in a cozy office complex in Orinda, California, AXA Rosenberg is a research and money management company with more than 240 employees worldwide, with offices in London, Hong Kong, Tokyo, and Singapore. Almost 60 of these employees spend all or part of their time programming. Then again, what would you expect from an organization whose foundation is quantitative analysis?

The company seeks to deliver "alpha," a measure of risk-adjusted outperformance, and optimize portfolios to meet preset goals. "When you have good alpha," says Bill, "it's a lot easier to market. The money almost comes to you. People feel more confident about what you are telling them." As part of its mission, the company uses sophisticated research models to build diversified portfolios designed to outperform a particular benchmark, such as the Russell 2000 Index, or MSCIEAFE Index, without assuming more risk than the benchmark. "We are effectively building a framework to capture the knowledge and expertise that an analyst or an investment manager brings to the day-to-day analyses of securities, going through financial statements and ultimately making a decision to buy or to sell," says Kenneth Reid, co-founder and global chief investment officer.

As a consultant at Barra from 1981 to 1986, Kenneth's work consisted of estimating multiple-factor risk models, designing and evaluating active management strategies, and serving as an internal consultant on econometric matters in finance. Prior to Barra, he earned a bachelor's and a multidisciplinary degree from Georgia State University, followed by a Ph.D. from the University of California at Berkeley, where he was awarded the American Bankers Association Fellowship. Now he has responsibility for the oversight of investment implementation across all portfolios around the world. His Ph.D. dissertation was incorporated into the firm's valuation and trading systems.

Naturally, at AXA Rosenberg, there is not a reliance on star managers to build strong performance; the models and the process are the stars. Research is conducted and the recommendations of the models are implemented by teams that openly share ideas and findings with a common goal of improving and enhancing a single investment process.

Portfolio Construction

Models comprising the investment process employ the same techniques that a solid, fundamental investor uses in selecting stocks. They have 500 to 600 stocks, on average, in each U.S. small-cap portfolio, and each one is selected based on its current relative value and earnings potential. And they are quick to sell stocks as soon as they reach fair value, with no second thoughts. Turnover of stocks within a portfolio is about 100 percent per year.

Since the company is hired to beat a benchmark—not time the market—portfolios typically have very little cash on hand. "We want every dollar invested to maximize return," says Steve. "On average, our cash position tends to be less than 1 percent of total assets, and is used mostly for the purpose of meeting shareholder redemptions." To build its portfolios of small stocks, the company selects from a universe of 5,000 securities in the United States and 17,500 globally.

"We don't have the same kind of insights into the management and business model that a qualitative investor has, but a qualitative manager typically won't be invested in as many companies," says Bill. "Ours is a totally different approach, but the logic, passion, the goal is the same." AXA Rosenberg sometimes says "we are not passionate about individual stocks, but we *are* passionate about our process." The model, Bill says, provides a ranking of stocks based on predicted return that is continually updated. For example, if the company buys a stock when its predicted return is 20 percent above the market, and six months later, the predicted return is zero, they will sell the stock and replace it with another company with better growth prospects. "We don't, however, just buy the stocks with the highest predicted returns," Bill points out. "We want the portfolio to look a lot like the benchmark it is trying to beat, in terms of risk characteristics. As a result, we select stocks that have, in our judgment, solid growth prospects and will complement the other holdings in the portfolio."

AXA Rosenberg was founded by Dr. Barr Rosenberg, whose name in research and money management circles has become quite legendary—not only for his success as an investment advisor but also for the relatively unconventional manner in which he achieved this success.

After earning a bachelor's degree from the University of California at Berkeley in 1963, and a Master of Science degree from the London School of Economics in 1965, he earned a Ph.D. from Harvard University in 1968. From 1968 to 1974, Barr taught finance, economics, and econometrics at University of California's School of Business Administration at Berkeley. Concurrently, he was a consultant in applied decision theory in the areas of banking, finance, and medicine and founded the Berkeley Program in Finance. He earned the reputation throughout the world as an expert in the modeling of complex processes with substantial elements of risk. In 1975, he founded a consulting firm, Barra. As managing partner and chief investment scientist, Barr would calculate betas (the volatility measurement of a security or a portfolio of securities in comparison with the market as a whole) for all stocks and act as consultant to money managers.

Moving from risk modeling to valuation modeling, Barr and three partners founded Rosenberg Institutional Equity Management 1985 to manage broadly diversified equity portfolios. He and Kenneth handled the research modeling, while Marlis Fritz signed on as the marketing partner and spearheaded the effort to sell the "process" to prospective investors

(Marlis retired from the company in 2002). A fourth partner, C. Richard Bartels, Jr., handled business development in Japan and offshore funds; he left the firm in 1989.

"The early days of business development were challenging and exciting," according to Marlis. "Since Barr was well known through Barra, many plan sponsors were willing to meet with us, curious to hear about what we were doing. At the time, active quantitative strategies were relatively new and buyers of investment services were not comfortable with the jargon, so we developed analogies to help us explain and demystify the strategy to the typical investment officer. In the early days, Barr never thought the company would ever be bigger than, perhaps, a couple dozen people. But as more prospective investors became familiar with our value-added process, he saw that there was a genuine need to develop an expansion strategy."

Given the firm's heavy emphasis on quantitative research, Barr and his partners grew the business by focusing on professionals with strong programming skills. During the first few years of the company's existence, most professionals had to take a programming test just to be considered for employment at the firm. And everyone who wanted to become part of the organization had to do more than just meet Barr's high standards. "You had to fit in with the culture," recalls Bill. "One thing was certain—if you were hired, you definitely became part of a close-knit family.

"When I joined the firm in 1989, the entire firm would participate in off-site meetings twice a year, in destination spots such as Pebble Beach and Carmel," recalls Bill. "We would have working sessions over two and a half days, exploring issues important to the firm as well as issues that were important to us as individuals. We talked about ways to make improvements and grow the business, but we also spent plenty of time discussing our personal lives and our professional ambitions. For many individuals, these personal discussions brought issues to the surface that were very emotional. But they proved to be extremely valuable as members of the AXA Rosenberg team."

America may be the land of opportunity, but few companies in the early stages of their development, particularly those in the financial services industry, can make the claim that they enjoyed immediate, sustainable success soon after swinging open their doors for business. That was the case for Barr, Kenneth, Marlis, and Rich when they set up shop in 1985. Even though they had no record of investment results, many individuals and institutions were willing to give them money to invest based solely on the reputation Barr had developed as a researcher in the academic and consulting world. Marlis recalls, "We had some wonderful early clients who took a leap of faith based on their confidence in Barr. But ours was a complex process that had to be validated by actual performance before most prospects took a serious look."

Over their first four years, they outperformed the broader market by 4 percentage points annually, and the money continued to flow in. The firm saw its total assets under management go from literally zero to nearly $10 billion, approximately $4 billion of which was from Japanese investors through a joint venture with Nomura. Behind the success was a system that Barr and his colleagues had created—a proprietary research and investment approach that could determine the true value of a company by conducting an exhaustive and highly sophisticated quantitative analysis of its inherent features in relation to its prevailing price. Back then, no one had confidence that such a system could succeed. And rightly so. "With equities, there's no ending to the number of features that could be analyzed to make the research meaningful and consistent over time," says Bill. "Unlike bonds, which may have five or ten sets, stocks have hundreds of features.

"At first, comprehensive, detailed analyses of hundreds of companies seemed far too complicated and complex to be reduced to a systematic, quantifiable system. Certainly a more practical and 'do-able' alternative would have been to look at earnings or book value since there is a definite association between prices in these features. But after careful consideration, we concluded that it was much too naive to employ this approach. "We asked ourselves, how many analysts actually consider hundreds and hundreds of items for thousands and thousands of companies? It's one thing to say, I am going to spend a week in this room and get my arms around this one company; it's another to say I am going to make simultaneous comparisons on 6,000 companies at that same level of detail. In the end, we knew that because our process was computer-driven, it would be straightforward for us to look at the level of detail that an individual investor might consider if he or she had the time, but to extend the analysis to consider all companies in our universe at the same point in time in an entirely consistent manner." This approach proved to be the foundation for what may appear to be continued success.

"Outperforming the market seemed so easy," recalls Kenneth. "To say that it was quite an enjoyable period for us would be a gross understatement. Back then, we were a relatively small group of professionals bringing in lots of assets and exceeding clients' performance expectations with great consistency."

"The demand for new, innovative products that existed during our early days also proved beneficial to the company," recalls Bill. "We proved ourselves early, and did not stumble. If you had the performance, you could walk into a final presentation, present your numbers, and there was a good chance you would win the account, even if your client did not fully understand the strategy. Today, well into our second decade, we have succeeded over the long term but have experienced disappointments along the way. As the industry has matured, the marketing process is just as important as strong long-term performance. It involves more than just phone calls and face-to-face meetings. You have to develop extensive, sophisticated commentaries and papers that present the models and the products clearly, in their best light, so that they can be used by the external team of experienced marketers and client service personnel."

Refining the Approach

By 1990, Rosenberg and his colleagues hit a peak of around $10 billion under management. Suddenly, the U.S. stock market came under pressure amid a severe recession in corporate earnings. Total assets under management abruptly began to decline—first due to market depreciation, then via withdrawals as investors began heading for the exits. But most of all, the spiraling Japanese markets resulted in $4 billion in redemptions as investors needed to show more cash. "In the U.S., earnings declined quarter after quarter for almost three years," recalls Kenneth. "So the market shifted sentiment totally toward companies that could sustain earnings, and avoided corporations with any hint of delivering a potential earnings disappointment to investors. That meant growth stocks were in and value stocks were out of favor with investors. Since our valuation model, at that time, was closely aligned with the value view of the world, we began to underperform. What made it worse was that investors, for whatever reason, were no longer evaluating corporations based on their inherent fundamentals." By the time the bleeding stopped, the company had seen its total assets under management drop from $10 billion to as low as $2.5 billion.

"It was a painful period, but instead of wondering whether this would be the end to a great run," recalls Bill, "we asked ourselves what refinements we might make to our approach while, at the same time, remaining true to our core beliefs and principle." As part of its ongoing learning experience, the team responded with clear ability, and produced a world-class product that is both forward looking and robust. "We responded with a flurry of research initiatives that led to the creation of strategies that enabled us to be competitive in both value and growth environments."

AXA Rosenberg uses two distinct models when evaluating approximately 17,500 stocks around the world. The valuation model evaluates price relative to everything known about a company. These details, which number hundreds, include balance sheet and income statement items, footnotes, and more. The intent of the model is to identify securities whose current valuations do not reflect their intrinsic worth. "The valuation model," says Bill, "looks at a variety of factors about the company to determine if there is an inconsistency between its current price and everything we know about the company. This is what all smart investors are trying to do. The question is, 'For this price, what do I get?'" For each of the companies the model follows, AXA Rosenberg has an estimate of what it believes the company is worth today, compared to its price. The valuation model doesn't include so-called forward-looking analytics. It simply provides what is known about the company and determines what it is worth on a given day.

The research is quite exhaustive. "All told, we have about 170 different business lines that we value," Bill adds. "For example, we don't look at General Electric as one company with one earnings number. To determine its value, we look at how it performs in the ten different industries in which it operates, relative to its competition, in order to realize its true value. That's a level of detailed analysis most people, in our judgment, just don't get to. Most investors and portfolio managers do not have an opinion on as many companies as we follow. What's more, most do not look at anywhere near the number of features in their analysis that we do. Others will produce opinions on companies based on particular variables. Our intensive research involves several hundred variables for each company." Bill points out that the valuation model is dynamic, operating in near-real time. For example, if today the market is paying more for the assets of retail food distribution companies than it pays for, say, IT (information technology) hardware companies, the model sees the change in valuation and adjusts it accordingly.

To describe how the valuation model is recalibrated to account for market dynamics, Bill uses the following real-estate analogy: "If you had a real estate agent or appraiser who went out and appraised property you might say, 'you appraised this property a year ago and it was twice as high as it is now. What's going on?' And the guy will tell you: 'Things have changed. I now look at the average square foot value in this neighborhood and it's down by 50 percent.' AXA Rosenberg does the same thing. A real estate appraiser could take a very quantitative approach like ours. He could take the price of all the homes that were sold and relate the characteristics of the homes to the price, and determine the current price for each characteristic and how it has changed over time. But real estate appraisers do it more informally, maybe less systematically. We are saying, okay, here are 6,000 prices today. Here are the characteristics of these companies. We run a regression analysis that tries to relate prices to these things. So the number is different every day."

When the market changed in the early nineties, AXA Rosenberg began working on a second way of analyzing stocks using an "earnings forecasting model," which projects the following year's earnings based on everything researchers know about the underlying corporation. This second model was completed in 1991, and put in place in the United States in the beginning of the fourth quarter of 1992. The earnings forecasting model performs a completely separate analysis of every company. Consisting of approximately 25 different variables, the earnings forecasting model is designed to determine what a company will earn next year. The earnings forecasting model effectively identifies companies that offer the most growth at the most attractive price by estimating earnings growth and dividing it by a company's current valuation," says Bill. "One of the variables in the model is the profitability of the company expressed as a return on equity (ROE)."

Adds Kenneth: "With the earnings forecasting model, we have a series of internally developed measures of higher price performance so we look back over the last five years at the different patterns of performance of a stock relative to the market and come up with a statistical measure of that prior price performance, and use that in predicting a company's future earnings."

Armed with the information from both of these proprietary models, AXA Rosenberg's models identify corporations that are reasonably valued and have good prospects for above-average earnings in the future. "In short," explains Bill, "the two models combine an intensive value approach with an equally intensive growth-at-a-reasonable price approach to identify the best securities to purchase at a given point in time. This combination helps give a portfolio fewer periods of negative performance because you've got two key insights into every company selected for investment."

A Culture of Intellect and Integrity

In 1999, Barr and his partners elected to sell the organization to AXA Investment Managers, a subsidiary of AXA SA, which owns 75 percent of the company—the remaining 25 percent is now owned by Barr and Kenneth. Assets as of late 2003 had topped $35 billion, with roughly 50 percent from the United States and Canada, and the rest from Europe, Japan, Asia, and Australia. "AXA Investment Managers seemed a wonderful partner for several reasons, Kenneth says. "For one, the company has the financial strength and stability to build on the foundation. Moreover, AXA has the resources to allow the team to focus specifically on what we do best—research—and to help in the distribution of products." When the firm completed the sale of a portion of its equity to AXA, Barr consolidated his research team into a separate entity that concentrates on the details of how the model selects stocks for purchase or sale.

Although the company is now part of a larger global organization, Steve says the culture is not much different than when Barr and Kenneth began building their team with 20 investment professionals, each of whom was well-versed in all facets of the business. "The collegial culture is similar to what you would find in an academic environment," says Steve. "There is still a focus on academic purity and research and the intellectual integrity of the models. In addition, there is a strong emphasis on individual effort. The integration of the company into AXA has worked out well. The company allows us to do what we do best without weakening our culture. In all, we are much better and far stronger today and, more important, our clients will be better off because of it. Our team members know that their ideas will be not only heard, but given serious consideration. And it applies to just about everyone—from engineers and computer scientists, to physicists and mathematicians. We're always looking for great ideas."

PART IV

, , ,

Global and Foreign Mutual Fund Managers

CHAPTER ELEVEN

BILL WILBY

OPPENHEIMER
GLOBAL
FUND

> > >

*T*alk about a worldly person; in many ways, our planet is just not big enough for Bill Wilby. He has lived on three continents, served internationally in the Army, and now leaves no stone unturned—anywhere in the world—as he runs the number-one global mutual fund, according to *Winner's Circle* research.

Bill is head of global investing at OppenheimerFunds, Inc., where he either manages or oversees 14 international funds. He has been working at the New York–based mutual fund company since 1992, and has more than 22 years of experience in the financial services industry. As his team at OppenheimerFunds includes five other portfolio managers and three securities analysts, Bill does less traveling today than he did earlier in his career. But he still spends plenty of time visiting companies outside the United States and interviewing executives of non-U.S. companies who pass through New York, where he is located. In addition, the managements of these international companies visit OppenheimerFunds' offices regularly, since the Global Fund usually shows up on their list of largest shareholders.

Bill is not your typical money manager. Unlike most investment professionals, he becomes more nervous when the stock market is going through a strong upward trend than when it is experiencing a sustained downturn and most investors are heading for the exits. "When the market is up," he says, "I'm more focused on how to protect my shareholders. But when the market is down, I feel I have new investment opportunities to look forward to, along with the anticipation of the market's next move forward." Being different, however, has its rewards. In the 10-year period through 2003, the team has an average annual return of 11.39 percent, almost double that of its benchmark, the MSCI (Morgan Stanley Capital International) World Index, at 6.93 percent, and more than 5 percentage points better than his median competitor.

Most spectacular about Bill's investing capabilities is his ability to navigate different market environments, and offer superior returns with less risk than his peers. For example, in the five-year period ending in 2003—through a bull market, bear market, then another bull market—he offered investors annualized returns of 10.05 percent, versus his average competitors' return of 0.37 percent (in the Morningstar world equity category) and a loss of 0.05 percent for the MSCI EAFE index.

A Worldly Beginning

Born in New Orleans in 1944, Bill was a military brat who attended 10 schools in 12 years. His earliest memory is sailing on a troop carrier with his mother across the Pacific Ocean in 1946. They were going to Japan to join his father, an army engineer in charge of building the Misawa Airbase, about 600 miles north of Tokyo. Bill was two and a half years old and had yet to meet his father, who had served with the 81st Infantry Division in the Pacific Theater.

Bill first learned about equities from his mother, who had a serious interest in the market and spoke about stocks frequently. "That was very uncommon," he remembers. "Back then, few women followed the market; and that was doubly true of people in the military." Bill's father preferred bridge, an interest he shared with Bill's mother, a duplicate tournament bridge player. "They encouraged me to learn to play and, of course, because they wanted me to, I never did. It became one of my regrets in life," he says. "Many great investors play bridge."

Bill did listen to his parents when he thought about leaving Georgia Tech in his sophomore year to book passage as a merchant seaman going to North Africa. Realizing that their son had not yet found his passion and worried about his future, Bill's parents arranged for him to receive an appointment to West Point. "This presented me with a difficult decision because, for one, if you ever turn down an appointment to West Point, you never have the option to go again. Also, since my father, grandfather (Bill's grandfather was a former superintendent of West Point) and great grandfather had gone there, I had to decide whether to break four generations of tradition."

Bill did go to West Point, graduated in 1967 and stayed in the military for the next eight years, serving in Military Intelligence. He completed Ranger School in the fall of 1967 and served in Vietnam as a communications officer with the First Infantry Division (the Big Red One). He returned from Vietnam to serve two years in Washington, D.C. as aide-de-camp to the commanding general of the Army Security Agency (part of the super-secret National Security Agency). After leaving Washington, Bill spent four years in Germany, his last military assignment as the commander of a 300-man detachment, eaves-dropping on the Russian forces occupying Czechoslovakia. Over the course of his military service Bill was awarded two Bronze Stars, two Meritorious Service Medals, two Army Commendation Medals, eight Air Medals (for combat time in helicopters), and the Vietnamese Cross of Gallantry.

"Vietnam was the first time I began to save money," he recalls. Bill managed to accumulate approximately $5,000 because, as he says, "you get combat pay and never had anywhere to spend your money." Flush with cash, Bill decided it was time to build on the investment knowledge passed on to him by his mother. On his return from Vietnam he began to read books about stock market investing. With newfound confidence to start buying shares, he entered the market, but, unfortunately for him, stocks were early in the stages of the worst bear market since World War II. "I managed to quickly turn $5,000 into $3,000," he says. "I realized I had a whole lot more to learn."

Four years later, while he was still serving with in the military in Europe, the Army offered to fund a graduate program in economics at Harvard if Bill would return to West Point as a professor. But when he calculated the military commitments that would be involved by accepting, he decided it was time to break family tradition and pursue a career in the private sector.

Upon leaving the service in 1974, he moved to Austria and taught skiing in the winter, and worked as a tour guide for a British travel company in the off season. A year later, he returned to the United States and settled in Colorado, where he took another job as a skiing instructor. When the season ended, he felt it was time to get serious about his future. In search of a new job, Bill went to the Federal Job Information Center in Denver. While there, he noticed many of the international organizations like the IMF or the World Bank were looking to hire economists. Many of the jobs were in exotic places, such as Africa and Southeast Asia, appealing to his love of travel and adventure. "Plus I thought economics might help me understand bear markets," he adds, not to mention the opportunity to pursue a "path not taken," free of military commitments.

"For the first time, I felt motivated about a particular career," he remembers. Realizing, however, that he would need more education Bill visited the head of admissions at the University of Colorado, 30 minutes away in Boulder. Two months later, he was in Colorado's Ph.D. program. In just two years, Bill completed his coursework for both his masters and Ph.D. at Colorado University. From there, he served as a visiting professor for one year at Arizona's Thunderbird School, a graduate program in international business (while there, he was voted "Outstanding Professor" by the school's MBA students). He finished his dissertation on the Eurodollar market six months later, and then went to work as an international economist at the Federal Reserve in Chicago in September 1980. During this period, Bill also worked as a Visiting Professor of Finance at Northwestern's Kellogg School in nearby Evanston, Illinois.

In 1981 he turned down a full-time teaching position at the University of California at Berkeley, and joined Northern Trust Bank, one of the first U.S. banks to start investing outside the United States. "The Bank had launched two international funds, but they were not doing well because of a sharp increase in the value of the U.S. dollar," recalls Bill. At Northern Trust, Bill was responsible for instituting a hedging program for their international funds, which gave him exposure to the equity market. The job took Bill on numerous trips between Chicago and Banque Scandinave en Suisse in Switzerland, where the fund managers were located. The experience both rekindled a passion for stocks and convinced him that U.S. institutions could and should manage foreign portfolios. The bank bought his arguments, and dropped both portfolios in his lap.

The Early Years in Money Management

When he began his money management career, Bill was particularly interested in foreign investing, because, as an economist, he specialized in international economics, currencies, and international monetary policy, and was particularly fascinated with liquidity and how it moves stock markets.

Given his background in economics, Bill's early investment style was more top-down than bottom–up. This style begins by deciding country or regional allocations on the basis of macro events and market parameters, then seeks to identify the best companies within those regions or countries. During his early years in money management, the top-down approach proved rewarding, enabling him to register outstanding performance. When he left Northern Trust in 1986, one of his funds, the Northern International Equity Fund, was the number-one ranked international portfolio, up 121 percent for the 12-month period ending March 31, 1986. But as international investing grew in popularity during the 1980s, markets became more efficient and companies became more important than markets or countries.

"In the early 1980s, there were enormous valuation differences between markets. Holland would be selling at a price-earnings multiple of seven times while Japan would be selling at 40 times. It was easy to see where the good values might be found. But as the markets became more efficient through increased investor participation, the inefficiencies in the markets began to dissipate. Now, some 15 to 20 years later, we have essentially evolved into one world stock market whereby the national differences are almost irrelevant now."

Bill says trying to invest with a top-down approach is akin to multiple market timing. "It's hard enough to time one market, but imagine trying to time 30 markets, which is what you are doing in that game. It's become a loser's game." Today, Bill and his team employ a bottom-up investment approach, looking for sound, well-managed companies with attractive investment potential.

As Bill has invested more of his energy in becoming a bottom-up money manager, he has also realized the importance of embracing a buy-and-hold approach. Today, he views himself as an owner of stocks, not a trader of stocks. "I generally don't buy a stock with the thought, 'when it gets to a certain price, I am going to sell it,'" he says. "If you are continually changing the composition of your portfolio, there's no way you are ever going to know what's in it. It takes time to get to know a corporation—how it trades, how the company works, whether or not it's a good investment for the long haul. I've been working for OppenheimerFunds since 1992, and I think it probably took me one, maybe two, years before I really understood the way the company works—and I was on the inside. Imagine as an outsider how hard it is to get to learn what's going on in a company. Hence, the more you trade your portfolio, the more you are throwing out all the work you've done on a company."

When asked how he scours the planet for investing ideas, Bill, team leader for OppenheimerFunds' Global team, replies: "It helps to be part of a world-class team." He is referring to his colleagues, each of whom manage their own fund: Rajeev Bhaman manages the Oppenheimer Developing Markets Fund; Rohit Sah manages the Oppenheimer International Small Company Fund; George Evans manages the Oppenheimer International Growth Fund; and Frank Jennings, whom Bill refers to as "the only competitor I worried about before he came on board" and "one of the brightest global managers in the business," manages the Oppenheimer Global Opportunities Fund. Additionally, the portfolio managers work with several analysts.

Investing as a Business Owner

Bill and his team at OppenheimerFunds take a businessperson's approach to buying stocks. They analyze the fundamentals of each company under investment consideration the same way any businessperson would if he or she were going to buy the company. To find these ideas Bill and his team identify investment themes and then pinpoint the best stocks within those themes. A theme, Bill says, is an area of the market that, in his team's judgment, has some great long-term growth momentum behind it. "We have four broad themes we invest in," he explains, "mass affluence, new technologies, restructuring, and aging."

Bill defines *mass affluence* as the ability of consumers—particularly those in less-developed countries and the rising numbers of wealthy people in industrialized countries—to buy products that were previously unaffordable. *New technologies* include biotechnology, information technology, and security. Corporate *restructuring* encompasses industries in which companies are focusing their business by either exiting or divesting themselves from nonprofitable or non-core operations.

The *aging* of the general population, particularly in developed countries, is the fourth theme, which leads to areas such as drug companies, health care, financial services, leisure, and biotechnology. In the biotechnology area, Bill and his team bought the stocks of genomic companies like Millennium Pharmaceuticals, Incyte and others well in advance of the boom these stocks experienced in the late 1990s. "We caught the wave well in advance of the mapping of the human genome."

Bill says, "Our thematic approach narrows down our search to companies with strong multiyear revenue growth since our growth themes generally represent business areas that are expanding at a share of world GNP. Strong top-line growth is necessary for long-term earnings growth." Instead of focusing on the price-to-earnings ratio, Bill typically relies on a company's price-to-revenue ratio to determine the cheapness or richness of a stock "because earnings tend to be more volatile than revenue." He also seeks sustainable profit margins and the potential for a company to in-

crease its earnings faster than the market average over a 10- or 20-year period. "Typically, if a company is operating in one of our theme areas, and it
has the ability to defend its profit margins, its income should be able to
grow rapidly. Finally if it uses its capital wisely, its earnings per share should
also grow as well," he says. Another investing characteristic: "In order to
maintain healthy profit margins, we like companies that are in businesses
with strong barriers to entry."

Global Diversification

Diversifying among various companies in different countries is para-
mount to OppenheimerFunds' investment methodology. And they don't
just focus primarily on developed regions, such as North America, Europe, and Japan. They are equally focused on finding good investments in
South America, Southeast Asia, and other developing regions around the
globe. In fact, Bill's company-focused approach paid off during the Asian
economic crisis in 1997. "That year, our largest position in the Global
Fund was an Asian stock, Nintendo, and it rose 55 percent in dollar
terms that year, despite collapsing markets in both Asia and Japan."

The Oppenheimer Global Fund, the second-oldest global fund in the
mutual fund industry, like all the funds under Bill's supervision, makes
large bets on companies where the team's conviction is high, and generally owns those companies for a long time period, typically over three
years. Many companies in the fund have been there 5 to 10 years or
more. On average Bill typically invests in 100 stocks at any given point in
time, although two-thirds of the fund is usually concentrated in the top
35 companies. "It certainly simplifies the math when you own 100 companies," he points out. "For example, with a 1 percent position in a particular company, I can easily determine how much money that would be
relative to the size of my portfolio. I like to look for companies that are
at least the size of my fund in terms of market capitalization. Then a 1
percent position in the fund is the same as a 1 percent ownership stake in

the company. If it's a smaller company, I can take smaller positions. It keeps the focus very easy."

Bill continues, "Also, I don't want to follow a thousand companies. I can find winners within my universe of 100. First of all, it's a selected universe because I thought enough of these stocks to put them in the portfolio in the first place. Too many portfolio managers are continually throwing their vested intellectual capital in understanding a company out the window. They'll sell one company and replace it with a new one. You have to think in terms of owning companies, not buying and selling stocks. This helps to keep a long-term perspective." To keep tabs on companies outside his perennial favorites, he occasionally relies on a global quantitative model that OppenheimerFunds developed, which covers over 30,000 global stocks. The model scrutinizes companies on a regular basis for valuation characteristics, such as earnings growth and other valuations.

When Bill and his team invest in a company, they have a good idea of what they are buying. But Bill says it generally takes a few meetings with the executives of a company to understand their personality and character, and to develop a strong view about the business—where it is today and where it might be 5 or 10 years from now. Once Bill finds what he would like to own long-term, he tries to identify the best time to buy. "You've got to buy a stock well to achieve good relative performance over time," Bill likes to say. "You can buy a company with a great ten-year earnings trend, but if the stock is highly overvalued, you are not going to make much money on that stock."

But there's another reason Bill places great importance on buying at an attractive price. "Inevitably, you are going to make a mistake and purchase a stock that doesn't pan out. If you purchased a stock at an attractive price it helps to minimize your downside risk in the event the stock price tumbles. While there's no perfect formula for identifying an attractive price for a stock, Bill says that bad news on the company or a market downturn is usually the sort of thing that produces attractive valuations. As a consequence, the team likes to buy those stocks when news is bad rather than when the news is good. "It's our view that the only time you can buy a company well is when the news is bad. You can buy a company that you estimate will have a great ten-year earnings trend, but if you buy it up here," he says, with his forefinger extended above his head, "you're not going to make money for ten years. You also have to add a cushion for potential mistakes, which always occur in this business."

Bill continues, "Our sell discipline is based on whether we believe our initial analysis is incorrect. But we refrain from setting sell targets because we consider ourselves buyers—not sellers—of stock. We generally feel that if we buy a good company in a good business well, and own it for a long period of time, it will most likely prove rewarding. I believe people who buy our funds today will be glad they did so five and ten years from now."

A Thematic Approach

While Bill places great importance on the value of spreading risk among different securities, there have been times when the stock of a particular company has appreciated so much in value that it has represented a significant portion of a fund's total assets. A case in point is Qualcomm, a stock that Bill and team started buying in the mid-1990s but whose potential did not materialize until the end of that decade. The stock fit nicely in the new technologies theme. But the wait was well worth it. The firm's investment in Qualcomm grew from $100 million to nearly $1 billion during an approximate four-year period. "In one fund alone [the Oppenheimer Global Fund], Qualcomm represented more than 13 percent of total assets during the late 1990s," Bill recalls. "I don't think any stock ever represented a greater portion of total assets than Qualcomm, but then we never owned a stock like this one."

Indeed, the Qualcomm experience is a unique story; this caught their

eye within the new technologies theme. "In the mid-1990s, our team became intrigued with CDMA technology, the technology used by Qualcomm for its cell phones. At the time, there was a huge controversy
between GSM technology, the standard in Europe, and CDMA. "But we
felt the attributes of CDMA were superior for service providers. Data
compression was better. There was less interference from adjacent frequen-
cies and fewer dropped calls. It was cheaper to install the antennas. And
perhaps most important, we had firsthand experience that convinced us
CDMA was better."

Back in the early 1990s the only real issue was whether or not CDMA
worked. One of the team's portfolio managers at that time visited South
Korea's Shinsegi Telecom, the first company in the world to use CDMA
technology in its cell phones. "The manager reported that the quality of
Shinsegi's wireless product was the best he had ever heard. It not only
worked, it worked great." Bill and his partner, Frank Jennings, concluded
that if CDMA ever became the standard for cell phones, Qualcomm
would benefit immeasurably because it owned the patents. At the time the
research was conducted, Qualcomm's stock was depressed, so Bill decided
the buying opportunity was ripe. When Bill and his colleagues established
a position in Qualcomm in 1995, their original entry cost was around $4
per share. They eventually bought around $100 million of Qualcomm
stock at these prices and waited.

"We watched the stock for four or five years, waiting for it to break out
in a big way. It was very frustrating as it went sideways for a long time," Bill
recalls. (Bill credits Frank Jennings for keeping him in the stock.) "Then in
1999, the International Telecom Standards Bureau decided on a form of
CDMA for third-generation systems and Qualcomm reached an accom-
modation with Ericsson (which had owned GSM, a European standard)
and the stock took off. Things started to happen. CDMA was not only
booming in Korea, it was being implemented in Japan, and other regions
were looking at the technology. Verizon Wireless started to take market
share in the United States, as well as Sprint PCS—both of whom used

CDMA systems. And AT&T was having problems with its TDMA technology because of frequent dropped calls on their system. Qualcomm took off and went up 26 times in 1999; at that point, we sold most of it by the end of 1999 and early 2000."

Bill and Frank sold large positions in Qualcomm, close to $1 billion worth of stock between July and December 1999. The stock price was soaring during that period and was arguably the hottest stock on the street when one analyst at a major brokerage firm gave Qualcomm a price target of $1,000 per share ($200 post-split). Soon after that firm made its optimistic call on Qualcomm, the stock split four to one. And not long after the split, Qualcomm began to slide sharply with the rest of the technology sector. By the summer of 2002, the stock was selling for just $23 per share, and true to form, both Bill and Frank began to buy the stock back.

Looking for ideas in the mass affluence and restructuring themes, Bill also gives credit to Frank for the team's purchase of Porsche stock in the mid 1990s. "At the time, Porsche was coming out of bankruptcy," he recalls. "We were impressed with management and intrigued by Porsche's new model, the Boxster. We felt the design was brilliant and well suited for the 40-somethings and nouveau riche in the United States.

In addition, because Porsche is a not a manufacturer—they outsource most production—they had very little capital invested in the business relative to other auto companies. "In effect, we essentially considered it an engineering and design company," Bill says. "And at that time, these companies were selling at P/E ratios of 25 or 30 times earnings, but Porsche was selling at around six times earnings. We could also see the psychology changing toward the company. And we knew if the psychology ever changed, the stock would likely go up." Not missing an opportunity, the team invested heavily, and has been the largest shareholder since the mid 1990s. The average cost of the position is around $62; the stock recently traded six times higher.

Some of Bill's other winners over the years were Nintendo, the Japanese

Game software company, Sanofi the French drug company, which also appreciated substantially during the 2000-2001 bear market; and Gilead Sciences.

A Collective Effort

To be a successful long-term investor, Bill says it is important to have a highly qualified team of professionals who can help find truly outstanding companies with superior growth potential. At Oppenheimer-Funds, Bill doesn't have a huge staff of analysts located in various areas around the globe. But his colleagues are very talented and highly experienced, and they believe in the importance of teamwork. "Every person on the team has certain strengths and weaknesses, but most importantly, they recognize them, which facilitates an easy working environment. For example, if one team member is strong in one area where others are not, he is likely to have a strong say with regard to investments there."

Bill likes to use superlatives when discussing his team. In fact, he attributes much of his success to his colleagues at OppenheimerFunds. "If I were out on my own since 1992," he says, "I'm not sure I would have been as successful as I've been. Many of us worked together before we joined the company. So my colleagues are more than business associates; they are friends, many of whom know more than I do when it comes to investing." (During the interview, Bill repeatedly commented on the team's strong culture of sharing ideas, and jointly learning together. He says: "I have to give adequate credit to my colleagues, without whom I would not have been as successful.")

As Bill reflects on his long and successful career, he says managing assets for other people has been not only financially satisfying but personally rewarding. For example, "When I meet someone who says, 'I've been invested in your fund for 10 years, and it helped me put my child through college,' I can't help but feel good about that. Money management is a very rewarding profession. Of course, given the sharp downturn in the equity markets over the past couple of years, there is also a painful side to this business. When someone says, 'I bought one of your funds at the top of the market and I'm now down 20 or 30 percent,' I feel terrible about that as well."

However, with times as difficult as they are today, Bill isn't nervous at all. In fact, the mood of the market is exactly the way he likes for investing. "The long-term investment opportunities are taking shape before us," he says. "Individuals who establish positions in fundamentally sound companies today will be happy they did so ten years from now."

CHAPTER TWELVE

JEFF EVERETT

TEMPLETON
FOREIGN
FUND

,,,

*W*hat is the best way to become a star in the world of investing? Try learning from a legend.

Jeff Everett worked side-by-side legendary investor Sir John Templeton, the dean of international investing, for nearly four years. Empowered with the investment philosophy and the accompanying discipline that Templeton finely tuned over the course of five decades, Jeff is proud that he has continued the legacy of providing outstanding returns to fund shareholders since taking the reins of the $14 billion Templeton Foreign Fund (as of year-end 2003).

Intense Training

"Learning from one of the greatest investors of all time, it was like I was earning my MBA, CFA, and Ph.D. all at once," Jeff says proudly. Indeed, the value-based, long-term philosophy that Sir John—as he is still affectionately known at Franklin Templeton—imparted on his student is deeply ingrained forever. "I don't make a move without first thinking, 'What would Sir John think about this?' "

The training wasn't for the lighthearted. Six months after joining the Templeton organization in late 1989, and three years after graduating Penn State in 1986, Jeff moved to Nassau to work with Sir John. Jeff lived in a small cottage, with little modern-day conveniences, and worked night and day. "I ate, drank, slept, and breathed the markets, geopolitics, and anything else Sir John would teach me," he reminisces. "I never considered it work because I knew it was exactly what I wanted to do with my life, and who I wanted to study under. I loved every moment." In addition to his grueling hours as an analyst, Jeff managed to find time to finish his CFA, or Chartered Financial Analyst, designation. Jeff laughs, then says: "At times it was like drinking from a fire hose."

Sir John is famous for recognizing value, and clearly his investment in Jeff paid off quickly. Jeff was a rising star; he covered 80 companies as an analyst, and earned his first managed account after two-and-a-half years. But it wasn't just any account. The $400 million account Jeff earned in 1991 belonged to Sir John's best friend. The account was also one of the firm's first, the sixth to be exact. Jeff still manages the account, which is now—without additional contributions—approaching the $1 billion mark.

In 1992, Sir John sold Templeton to Franklin Resources and retired, devoting himself to philanthropic and spiritual causes. At this time Jeff worked under Mark Holowesko, who was also trained under Sir John. In 1995, opportunities for Jeff arose when a portfolio manager left the firm; Jeff was offered the opportunity to manage the Templeton World Fund, a fund that invests globally in value stocks, and co-manage the Templeton Foreign Fund, which invests in value stocks outside the United States. Overnight, the combined assets he was managing jumped from almost half a billion to over $8 billion. In 2000, Mark Holowesko left the Templeton World and Foreign funds to build the hedge fund group at Templeton; Jeff became chief investment officer for the global equity group and sole lead manager for both funds.

In a way, Jeff feels like he has been training for this job his entire life. He started thinking globally even as a child in Springfield, Pennsylvania. In his early teens he was fascinated about the world, reading anything he could get his hands on, always seeking to broaden his knowledge base. Out of pure interest he would (and still does) read magazines ranging from *Flying* to *Popular Science*, to boating and geopolitical publications. He's currently reading *War in the Time of Peace*, by David Halberstam (New York: Scribner, September 2001). He loves discussing diverse topics, with most conversations turning philosophical in nature. "The more I learn, the better able I am to formulate thoughts, not opinions. Opinions don't make you money in the markets, but thought plus fact can make you money. Sir John crystallized this thought process; you must look at things differently than the crowd." In fact, Sir John once said, "Buy at the point of maximum pessimism," referring to the act of buying solid, but undervalued companies when they are out of favor, and holding for the long term. This "way of thinking" is the real discipline behind Jeff's investment philosophy, enabling him to invest with a contrarian bent.

The Investment Philosophy

"Sir John has proven that global investing offers geographic diversification, as well as the optimum risk/reward profile," Jeff says. "We seek value wherever it can be found, without rigid geographic limitations. Country and industry weightings are residuals of the stock selection process; they do not drive it. This enables us to incorporate our best ideas into every portfolio throughout the portfolio construction process."

The investment philosophy is based on three rules: The first is thinking long-term. "One of Sir John's maxims is 'If you want better returns than the crowd, then you can't invest with the crowd,' " Jeff says, referring to his contrarian style. "One way to invest away from the crowd is to take a long-term approach to investing, which so few actually do." It is evident Jeff is no short-term trader. In fact, Templeton Foreign Fund's long-term turnover is typically 20 to 25 percent, meaning stocks remain in the portfolio for an average of around four or five years. This makes Templeton Foreign Fund far more tax efficient than its peers' average turnover of 88.7 percent (in the Morningstar foreign value category), meaning the average holding stays in the portfolio for little more than a year (currently, the Foreign Fund's turnover is 34 percent).

The ideal words to describe his long-term approach seem to be anticipation and patience. "I don't care what you do in life, whether it's sports, education, or investing, anticipation is a critical element. Being able to anticipate anything, which requires some intuition and some common sense, gives you the ability to look at the horizon for conclusions." Jeff illustrates by way of the adoption of cellular phone usage. "Cell phones are a tremendous market now, but the United States was far from leading the way. Cell phone usage took off very quickly in Europe, and to this day South Korea and Japan are the undisputed champions of mobile phone technology in terms of usage, penetration rates, and quality of service. I am required to look at trends and determine if they are transportable across boundaries and geographic territories.

"In our business, we anticipate by taking very broad perspectives, anticipating developments and advances that we extrapolate from one region to other regions around the world," Jeff continues. "When I spot a trend I want to know who will benefit, in terms of the regions and companies, why it will happen and when is it likely to materialize." Often, according to Jeff, patience is required, as trends may not materialize for years. But importantly, it is the companies benefiting from broad trends, not the broad trends, upon which they focus their energies at Templeton.

"As a buyer of undervalued securities," Jeff explains, referring to his second tenet, "whether the shares are undervalued due to a company restructuring or the industry is out of favor on Wall Street, it goes without saying that it takes time for the value to be restored to share prices as the company works out their problems. You need to be a long-term investor, especially if the stock goes down after you buy it—as long as your opinion remains intact, you have to wait it out or buy more shares at lower prices." Additionally, Jeff and the research team spend days, even weeks, developing prospective ideas for the funds, with long-term forecasts and models; "it's almost counterintuitive for us to not invest for the long-term.

"In today's environment, value investing generally means buying out-of-favor stocks, which almost by definition is contrarian in nature," he says. "We could also be considered contrarian because international investing is out of favor for a lot of people right now. Pursuing undervalued securities requires you to think like a businessman. That's why Warren Buffett is an extraordinary investor. He invests as a businessman. He likes to look at undervalued situations, he likes to buy brands that dominate in their markets, he takes a close look at management, and—as a businessman—he thinks long term."

During a company analysis, Jeff and team perform extensive due diligence to learn about the management team, including interviews and face-to-face meetings. While some great investors, such as Buffett, will pay a premium for top-notch management, Jeff considers management essential, but would rather wait for the right valuation than pay a premium.

Jeff recalls one mistake he made back in the late 1990s. London-based Cable and Wireless CEO Richard Brown quit the telecom firm after a series of mishaps, including a botched $1.7 billion acquisition, a formal SEC probe into an earnings warning, a $430 million troubled contract, and a stock that dropped from £12 a share to about £1. He reemerged as CEO of EDS, the world's second-largest provider of information technology services. At the start of 2002, when the stock was in the low 60s, the problems started: two investigations by the SEC, both involving Richard; an earnings warning and hedging activities around its stock that led to large losses; and a plunge in its share price. In early 2003, EDS's stock was in the mid-teens. Richard was ousted from EDS and Michael Jordan left his chairman position at CBS to become EDS's chairman and CEO. Although the contrarian in Jeff told him to buy more shares after the plunge, which eventually brought him to a breakeven status, he says he should have sold as soon as EDS brought in leadership with less-than-stellar credentials. "This is an example of how we are fine-tuning our approach, and clearly learning from our mistakes," Jeff admits.

Jeff describes the final rule: "At the end of the day, you can't directly invest in consumer confidence, unemployment figures, or consumer sentiment, but you can invest in Volkswagen. The third rule is to research the companies." This last rule underpins the bottom-up approach, or seeking the best undervalued companies before consideration of macro elements such as the economy or political events. While Jeff doesn't immediately concern himself with the macro issues, he takes advantage of what he calls "full-circle" analysis. He explains: "The whole business world can be compared to a food chain. We may hold insurance stocks, knowing that rates are increasing, and insurance is a growing expense for businesses. When we talk to companies, they should be confirming this. Similarly, if we discover a supply issue with a manufacturer, we know that the repercussions will be felt throughout the supply and distribution chain." As another example, Jeff learned about many U.S. companies moving functions to India: "Not outsourcing, but actually moving operations to India. Companies are acknowledging the cost benefits, which are around four-to-one, meaning you'll pay $20 an hour for a programmer instead of $80 in the United States. I see the same types of trends forming in Europe."

Seeking New Opportunities

Indian-company HDFC, or Housing Development Finance Corp., illustrates an investment Jeff made that met his three tenets. "How would you like to have bought Fannie Mae stock back at its infancy, knowing what you know now that the company's shares have had an extraordinary rise? HDFC is an example of a trend that we saw forming, and invested early. We grasped the trend, it is a business we understood, and a great place to be from a big perspective, and it has a strong management team. Many investors automatically think that companies in emerging markets must have substandard management—this couldn't be further from the truth! The company's chairman, Deepak Parekh, who, incidentally, I just met with before our interview, is a world-class manager.

"Deepak started the company in conjunction with the World Bank in 1977. The company is a private-sector housing finance company in India, and is considered one of Asia's best managed companies by several publications (*AsiaMoney* named the company 'Best Commercial Bank in India 2002;' EuroMoney awarded the company 'Best Bank—India' in 1999, 'Best Domestic Bank' in India in 2000, and 'Best Bank in India' in 2001 and 2002) and Deepak is considered one of Asia's finest managers."

Jeff was familiar with the company back in the eighties. "By traveling and talking to people around the world we're always learning of new opportunities," Jeff says. When Jeff first bought the stock for Templeton in 1990, the company had 700 employees (now 1150) and 24 offices (now 142), assets per employee grew 1,100 percent, and profits per employee grew 20-fold. Even in the bear market of the early 2000s, not including dividends the stock annualized a compound return of 32.6 percent from early 2000 through May 2003.

"We learn of opportunities, whether big or small, through our global reach," Jeff says. "This is one of the real advantages of working at a major firm with a major research department. It allows us to keep close tabs on hundreds of companies around the world. We spend tens of millions of dollars a year for our global research team, which includes 32 outstanding individuals located around the world, results in thorough analyses and due diligence, and new opportunities."

Due Diligence

When meeting with companies, Jeff is often told: "It's very interesting meeting with you because the questions you ask aren't like the ones a lot of other investors ask." Jeff prefers to stick with questions that will lead him to accurately forecast the company's future prospects. "Rather than discussing quarterly earnings or monthly sales, I'm more interested in, say, a company's capital expenditure plans or manufacturing plans for the next two to three years. Our questions are far more open ended about the future of the company, its industry, changes within its industry, and regulatory issues. Other questions will include: How is the industry changing? What could cause the next few years to be a disaster? What kind of demand will you see in an economic downturn? My questions may be a bit different than what the companies traditionally hear, but I need to feel as if I'm sitting in the CFO's chair."

He continues, "This all comes back to full-circle analysis." The data and analyses that Jeff collects are massive. After a recent trip to India, he returned home with four boxes stuffed with information from a single company meeting. "During a company visit a company may give us sales projections, and tell us they're going to make X number of plastic toothpaste tubes. After I synthesize the loads of data, I may conclude that there's no way they could attain those projections with their current capacity without building another factory. When you put the pieces together, like in a puzzle, with a long-term perspective, you produce interesting conclusions, and more often than not, our conclusions become a reality, even if it takes some time. This is a very important element in our approach and our discipline. Whether it's a company in a developed nation or emerging market, we perform this extensive analysis," he affirms.

Here's the procedure an analyst takes before he or she makes a stock recommendation: First, a very detailed set of financial projections is composed, based on a company's balance sheet, income statement, and cash-flow statements. "We always look at a company's potential for earnings and growth over a five-year period. If an analyst doesn't feel a particular stock is the right fit for one of our portfolios and they've done sufficient analysis, then it's on to the next one. From our standpoint, there's no stock in the world we think we must own." Analysts present candidate companies to their fellow analysts for review prior to placing them on a "Bargain List," a central point of the investment process and a tool used in constructing all of the firm's portfolios.

The analysts seek stocks that are cheap relative to their assets, cash flows (the average price to cash flow for the stocks in the Foreign Fund is currently 7.87), and earnings potential. Consequently, the fund's average price-to-earnings multiple is 15.55 and price-to-book ratio is 1.55, both extremely low compared to its peers. Consequently, Jeff has been exposed to industries, such as energy and financial stocks, that traditionally meet his undervalued status. (Currently, his biggest sector holding is financial services, with 29.9 percent of the portfolio's assets, followed by industrial materials, with 25.16 percent of assets.)

Investing Away from the Crowds

Jeff compares these days to the early 1990s, when investors avoided the financial stocks. "People don't buy financial stocks during a recession, when interest rates are in the double digits," as they were in Europe, Jeff says. "But the valuations already discounted these high interest-rate levels. It was already accounted for in the price of the stocks. We knew we'd come out of the recession, and interest rates would drop; we just didn't know exactly when."

In 2002, after the technology bubble burst, Jeff began buying beaten-down technology stocks, such as South Korea's Samsung Electronics. In 2003 he started buying the beaten-down telecom stocks. Then there was the time Jeff was aggressively buying during the Mexican peso devaluation of 1994; the U.S. recession of 1990; the Russian crisis of 1988; and far more that date back to the 1940s if you include Sir John's experiences, on which Jeff's philosophy is based. "This approach requires discipline, courage, patience, and the ability to discriminate between short-term noise and long-term trends and values," Jeff says. "We believe that by systematically removing emotion from investment decisions, our performance may benefit from the long-term efficiency of the market."

Clearly, Jeff will invest where others don't dare, finding value when investors are selling in a state of panic. On May 1, 1997, in the midst of a bull market in Hong Kong stocks, Jeff's thorough research and keen instincts led him to publish a research report that described his bearish outlook on the market, particularly the property sector. "Despite our buy-and-hold mentality, we constructively make decisions about what is overvalued and what is undervalued," Jeff says. "While the market can fluctuate pretty widely, pricing stocks cheap and expensive, our valuations change only when we feel the fundamentals of the company provide us compelling reasons to take action." Still, when Jeff sees investors either rushing to buy or panicking to sell, he will see dramatic differences between his target price and where the market is currently pricing a stock. He likens his approach of investing in the opposite direction of the crowd to an individual commuting against rush hour traffic in New York City.

In the 20-page report, Jeff identified areas that he believed character-ized a market top. For example, he believed that valuations were stretched, particularly the result of weaknesses in the financial systems. In his report he said: "There is no debate about whether the structural forces in Hong Kong are fundamentally sound—they are not." He con-tinued to describe concerns about corporate governance. In the prop-erty market, where Cheung Kong is a dominant player, Jeff described "core problems" with the government relating to "infrastructure and development" barriers. After he published his report in 1997, Jeff began selling Hong Kong shares. He sold much of the fund's shares in Cheung Kong at a price of about $79 a share.

Despite the negative signals Jeff published in his report, the bull mar-ket roared ahead; three months later, on July 1, markets soared even higher as the British relinquished Hong Kong to the Chinese; the next day, the Bank of Thailand allowed the baht currency to float, after it failed to defend the currency. This served to make its exports more competitive with those from China. In turn, other Southeast Asian countries—the Philippines, Malaysia, and Indonesia—felt pressure to devalue their currencies to stay competitive. Currency speculators jumped in, and as the Southeast Asian currencies depreciated, foreign capital flew out of their domestic markets, sending stock, real estate, and other markets tumbling. As much of Southeast Asia's highly acclaimed growth was financed by huge foreign investment, the devaluation of their currencies and subsequent flight of foreign capital left the hardest-hit Southeast Asian countries with stagnant domestic markets and piles of debt denominated in hard foreign currencies, which appreciated in local currency terms by huge percentages. The crisis was made worse by governance issues, notably government involvement in the private sec-tor and lack of transparency in corporate and fiscal accounting and the provision of financial and economic data. Western countries were in-creasingly concerned that the crisis would drag down the rest of the world economy.

On August 7, 1997, Hong Kong's Hang Seng index, the market's lead index, closed at a record high of 16,673.27, and shares of Cheung Kong climbed to $96 a share, over 20 percent higher than where Jeff sold the position. As the stock increased in value, Jeff's conviction that the stock was overvalued only grew stronger. Within two weeks the index dropped 1,200 points; a year later the index was 58 percent below its high. This particular situation seems to be characteristic of the Templeton approach: "We lost out on the additional 20 percent, but we missed out on the 70 percent fall."

Then the Asian crisis began. Within three months after the crisis began, the Dow Jones Industrial Average dropped around 600 points, and Jeff started buying back his Cheung Kong shares, as well as several other stocks. Jeff, who relies primarily on company research with little regard to macro events, started buying the stock again when the stock was knocked down to the upper 20s in August of 1998, and now has an average price per share in the low 60s. In fact, Templeton became the largest shareholder in Hong Kong, before the government stepped in and helped to stabilize the markets by buying shares. "We saw huge opportunity," he says. "We saw good businessmen running good businesses, with good balance sheets, with strong growth and great valuations. Within two years the stock tripled in price. As of February 20, 2004, the shares were trading at around $75.

"We value the relationships we have with Asian management teams, including Cheung Kong; these are relationships Templeton has developed over the decades. I am always upfront with them when I'm selling their shares, for example, and they're open with me when it comes to issues at the company—they appreciate the fact that we're upfront with them, and they, in turn, are straightforward with us. I would, however, agree that many Asian management teams suffer from a lack of focus, but these are mainly the large conglomerates." Cheung Kong Holdings "has one of the best managements in Asia, if not the entire world," Jeff says of his second-biggest holding, which is now around 2 percent of assets. "The company's founder, Li Ka-Shing, who is also the chairman of conglomerate Hutchison Whampoa, is really world-class, and has a long track record of successes and delivering great returns for its shareholders; in fact, the management team owns around 38 percent of the outstanding shares. Ka-Shing's performance in the 1990s was above 20 percent, on par with Warren Buffett's Berkshire Hathaway (the S&P, by comparison, was up 18.19 percent over the same time period). Every company we invest in has considerable focus on their business." Jeff then turns back to his esteem for Ka-Shing: "If you believe, as I do, that there will be a great bull market in Asia over the next decade, wouldn't you want to be in it with the Warren Buffett of Asia? Li Ka-Shing is a shrewd trader of businesses; he will see the opportunity and profit from it."

Jeff takes the accounting issues very seriously: "It's important to note that even during the Asian crisis, the fundamentals of the companies in which we were invested remained sound," he says. "We've delivered attractive returns for our shareholders because we invest in companies with management we can trust, fundamentals that are strong, and companies that are positioned to perform very well in their markets. "Asia has phenomenal demographics," he continues, "with the region having the biggest consumer-oriented economies in the world. Asia is currently capitalizing on western technological advances, which will facilitate even faster growth. Thirty years ago you wouldn't even recognize some of these Asian cities, such as Seoul. Even a decade ago you wouldn't recognize the quality product South Korea builds. Their cars are high quality, at a very low cost. Their cellular phone technology is incredible," Jeff says, referring back to his previous example. "It's amazing to me that these countries now run circles around us in certain areas."

Jeff continues, "South Korea is a country that transformed itself from being a tremendous debtor nation, to one that paid off all its IMF (International Monetary Fund) loans, to becoming a nation with a big surplus in its budget—all since the Asian crisis began in 1998. Additionally, the country has introduced significant transparencies in regard to its governance.

The country is welcoming foreign investors with open arms; for example, a group called Carlyle bought into a major bank and General Motors bought assets from Daewoo. This is a major improvement in the way they treat foreigners.

"One of my favorite stories is Samsung Electronics. In the late 1990s, during the Asian crisis, few wanted to own a stock like Samsung. Yet it is one of the most profitable companies in the world. On a net basis, the company earned $7 billion in 2002; this compares to $3.6 billion for IBM. Samsung's market cap is currently only $47 billion, compared to IBM's $148 billion; Samsung has no debt, and is sitting on $6 billion in cash on its balance sheet. It is a tremendous powerhouse with products that have become far more quality oriented and more compelling compared to its competitors'.

"This region of the world is truly remarkable," Jeff continues. "In the 1970s everything in Japan was low quality; products broke easily. In the span of 30 years, Japan has become a high-tech, high-quality manufacturer of consumer electronics. Korea experienced the same type of metamorphosis, except it accomplished the changes in the period of 15 years. There's one major difference between these two countries: Japan was never really an open economy, with the large companies controlling the market; Korea started like that, but now Korea is letting in the foreigners, while Japan still isn't."

While Jeff looks around the world for the best values, Asia in particular fits the mold for the Templeton philosophy. "When assessing valuations for the long term, Asia in our opinion shows some of the most attractive value opportunities," he says. "I'm somewhat agnostic when it comes to the country we invest in because I limit my analyses to the companies, but when I consider the demographics and long-term trends on the company level, I'm surprised there aren't more outside investors putting money to work in Asia—that just makes it even more attractive to me." Jeff comments on investors' preoccupation with the soaring markets in the United States from the 1980s to early 2000s. "During the market peaks in the United States, many foreign investors were asking us what hot technology stocks they should invest in," Jeff says with a smile. "That was the same time we were avoiding those stocks."

As events—such as the Asian crisis—unfolded, it seemed only to reinforce the beliefs Jeff learned from Sir John and in his own personal experiences. "Many U.S. investors have shunned the world markets, including the Asian markets. This is primarily because of their perception of foreign companies as having sub-par management with a lack of focus, corporate governance issues, and transparency concerns regarding accounting," Jeff says, preparing to counter these issues.

"To start, it's important to recognize that just because investors don't have investments overseas doesn't mean they don't share some of the risk," Jeff comments. "Just because you didn't own Korean stocks during the Asian crisis doesn't mean you could hide from it. Same with the Russian and emerging markets crises in 1998; if you are in U.S. stocks, then you felt it to some degree. More recently, some of the Asian markets were affected by the SARS outbreak. Investors in the U.S. markets felt it as well—you can't be completely immune from it. With the corporate governance issues, U.S. investors are feeling a bit hypocritical now that we've felt the collapsing of ethics on our turf. At least in Asia we knew we had to watch out for it; in the United States, not even our regulators had a clue. And this comes at a time when the Asian markets are opening up to foreign investors."

How passionate is this *Winner's Circle* mutual fund manager about investing globally? "As with any asset class, international investing should play an important part in an investor's asset allocation and diversification plan," Jeff begins, referring to his niche in general, not to mention the 50-year track record both Sir John and Jeff have maintained with their irrefutable investing philosophy. "Whether an individual invests with us or somewhere else, I urge them to take a look at the opportunity. Today it's easy to participate with the proliferation of international mutual funds, directly through a domestic brokerage account or through an account that can be opened with an international securities firm.

"What investors are understanding more each year is that even if they do not own overseas stocks, preferring the safety of their home market—in this case, mostly in the United States—even the U.S. stock market can and will be influenced greatly by overseas geopolitical and economic developments." Never was this more evident than in 1998, when the combination of the Asian crisis, Russian crisis, Long Term Capital Management, and "near-miss" Brazilian crisis conspired to drive stocks to their September 1998 lows.

Though Sir John's philosophy is timeless, and a proven success for many decades, Jeff is constantly seeking ways to improve it. "Like a long-time winning football team, its fans expect the team to continue its track record," Jeff says. "Their expectations are always being raised. Investors expect a certain degree of excellence from us, and we're determined to deliver." Jeff pauses to emphasize his next point: "I'm just fortunate to be building on one of the greatest investment philosophies of all time. I know that in the short-term investors may wonder what we're up to," he says, laughing at how incongruous—regardless of his accuracy—some decisions may have seemed. "But in most of these cases, valuations simply don't reflect accurate analyses," Jeff says with pure conviction. "These inaccurate valuations reflect an undue element of emotion and short-term fears that will be corrected over time."

In Jeff's view, "Whether there's a bull market or a bear market, there are always tremendous opportunities if you have a long-term outlook. When we put together research, our conclusions may not be realized for 6 or 12 months or even longer. We have the discipline, but investors need an element of discipline as well. Too many investors will see their investments aren't working in the short term, and they act at the exact wrong times. Unfortunately, the short-term horizon of investors was one of the major obstacles to their success during this recent bear market. Whether bear market or bull market, we're always going to spot opportunities, and we're always going to be patient as our convictions come to fruition. You can't call yourself a value investor unless you are patient."

How strongly does Jeff believe in his philosophy and in Franklin Templeton? He does not hold a single stock outside the company. "The fact that I get paid to do something I love is incredible to me," he says in a quieter voice, leaning forward. "My entire life savings, as well as most of my relatives' and friends', is on the line with our investors."

While Jeff's philosophy requires a discipline that is void of emotions, his spirit seems to be elevated from the personal relationships he has developed with scores of financial advisors and investors. "It is a tremendous privilege to help every single one of our millions of shareholders."

PART V

, , ,

Sector and Bond Mutual Fund Managers

CHAPTER THIRTEEN

SAM ISALY

EATON VANCE
WORLDWIDE
HEALTH
SCIENCES FUND

❯ ❯ ❯

*S*am Isaly's incredible success managing Eaton Vance Worldwide Sciences Health Fund is nothing short of extraordinary. Over a 10-year period ending February 29, 2004 his fund generated an annualized return of 18.04 percent, far outpacing its peers'—the Dow Jones Healthcare Sector—performance by almost 2 percentage points. With this kind of performance, and a handle on risk, Sam is an easy frontrunner as a *Winner's Circle* mutual fund manager in the health care sector. Interestingly, his ability to think differently, and innovate, have been key to his success in managing the fund. In fact, it seems to run in the Isaly family.

The Beginning

His father and grandfather invented and made the first Klondike bar, which later became America's number-one selling ice cream novelty. Along the way, the family bought 11 milk plants and eliminated the middlemen by opening up dairy stores and delicatessens in the Midwest to sell their products. By the 1950s, the Isalys owned over 400 of these stores—not bad coming from a man who started by selling milk from a wagon.

Unfortunately, Sam became close with his father only through stories told by others; his father died soon after Sam's first birthday. Sam and his mother became very close, and he marveled at how she raised four children, how she managed her finances, and, in particular, her investing prowess.

Sam knew at an early age that he wanted to be a successful business-man. He studied hard in school, earning top marks through high school, and competed determinedly in athletics. Then, at the age of 18, the un-thinkable happened. During a wrestling match, Sam suffered a spinal cord injury, leaving him in a wheelchair for the rest of his life.

Never one to succumb to obstacles, Sam pressed even harder, eventually being accepted to Princeton University, even as another Ivy league with-drew its offer after his accident. While there, he earned extra money watching the ticker tape and day trading his portfolio. Though he was suc-cessful with many winning trades that helped pay college bills, he later de-termined that the winning trades were a fluke: "I realized the market is way too efficient, and it was strictly gambling," he says.

In the summer of 1965, Sam apprenticed as a margin clerk for his mother's stockbroker. One of the firm's principals became impressed with the young Isaly's knack for investing, and gave him a copy of *Security Analysis*, the 1934 classic that immortalized its authors, Graham and Dodd, as the masters of fundamental securities analysis. Captivated, Sam could hardly put it down; in fact, decades later, he can still recite passages. The book changed his life. He knew his future was destined for Wall Street.

By the time he graduated with a major in economics in 1967, he earned the designations of Phi Beta Kappa and Magna Cum Laude, and was the first student in a wheelchair to graduate Princeton. Eager to hit the business world, his path was altered for the better when he learned that he won the prestigious Fulbright scholarship, an international educational program sponsored by the U.S. government designed to enhance interna-tional relations. The scholarship is given to students with exceptional lead-ership skills and academic achievements.

He attended the London School of Economics where he was further mesmerized by the financial markets. While there, he successfully specu-lated against the British pound. After he earned his masters in economics in 1968, Sam returned to the United States and landed a job in the trust department of Chase Manhattan Bank.

Finding a Niche

When he first arrived for work, he was told of a pharmaceutical analyst position that was open in the managed money area. "They told me they don't 'have anyone doing drugs,' " he recalls with a laugh. "I was a decent scientist with advanced-placement classes that I took in chemistry, biology, and physics; it sounded intriguing so I decided to accept the position."

As Sam's proficiency in analyzing and seeking attractive pharmaceutical investments escalated, more opportunities opened up for the rising star. He made his way to Paris, working for a large European investment firm seeking pharmaceutical companies worldwide. He later joined Merrill Lynch, leading their research efforts in the Far East.

In the early eighties, Sam decided that with the experience he had accumulated, he could set up his own business selling his independent worldwide research in pharmaceutical and biotechnology companies to institutional investors. His business was an instant success. His ability to spot promising startup and emerging companies globally was a niche that clearly differentiated him from any other researcher, and quickly caught the attention of the biggest Wall Street firms and institutional investors.

In 1989, Sam put his ideas to work by taking over a smaller mutual fund. As he was planning the fund, *Barron's* ran a story on Sam's successful research efforts, focusing on his global capabilities. A few days after the story hit the newsstands, a gentleman in Florida contacted Sam about managing a small fund that consisted of retired doctors' money; the doctors essentially started a fund, and combined their money and investment ideas. Sam decided that this was the simplest way to start a fund, as all the legal requirements were met and the flood of paperwork required and high costs to initiate a fund were taken care of. In August of that year, Sam officially became the portfolio manager for the Medical Research Investment Fund for his new company.

Sam immediately put to work his investment philosophy, the basis of which he says was really formed back in his days at Princeton. The biggest influence on his philosophy was the statement made by one of his professors, Burton Malkiel, that you can't beat the market because all information is already priced into stocks, a theory often referred to as the efficient market theory. Sam, however, felt he now had an edge over the market. "I could obtain extra information by using my approach on a worldwide basis," he says.

Sam didn't waste any time showing his skills: His performance was an immediate success, posting remarkable gains and ranking him as one of the best in the health care mutual fund sector. In fact, his outsized gains were so attractive that it caught the attention of mutual fund company Eaton Vance, which at that point did not have a health care fund. In 1996, Eaton Vance Distributors, Inc. became the distributor for the fund, and changed the fund's name to Eaton Vance Worldwide Health Sciences Fund. OrbiMed, LLC, which Sam founded in 1989, acts as outside advisor to the fund and now advises seven funds as an independent advisory firm and manages around $4.5 billion.

Perhaps the biggest difference between the philosophy he developed at Princeton and now is his infrastructure, which is capable of covering the pharmaceutical and biotechnology industries around the world. OrbiMed Advisors sports a research team that has more analyst coverage per investment than any other fund company in the United States. Sam, as managing partner, and his other three partners manage four biotechnology and pharmaceutical mutual funds, with an analyst team that currently includes 10 additional analysts—all with medical or business backgrounds. The analysts boast impressive resumes, including five with Ph.D.'s and a medical doctor; among the others, most have earned their MBAs, as well as designations including CPA and CFA, and one has a law degree. All told, 14 highly qualified professionals are combing the universe of around 600 companies; each individual closely follows about 20 stocks and has around four companies in the portfolio; Sam is the lone portfolio manager. "In general, we have profit-and-loss people, such as myself, and the technology-associated people, such as the molecular biologists," he says. "We think that both of these skills are necessary."

World-Class Research

Building a world-class research team was essential to Sam, as he never uses Wall Street research. He also required the proper infrastructure to obtain and process more information from companies located throughout the world. As of this writing, around 30 percent of the 40 to 50 companies that the portfolio is holding are typically located outside the United States, particularly in Europe, with 20 percent of fund assets (mostly in France and Germany), and Japan, with 9 percent of fund assets. Some of the European companies the fund currently holds include Swiss-based Novartis (with 4.8 percent of assets) and Serono S.A (4.10 percent); France-based pharmaceutical Sanofi-Synthelabo S.A. (3.5 percent); and Germany-based pharmaceutical Altana (3.8 percent). Japanese holdings include Takeda Chemical Industries Ltd., a pharmaceutical company with 3.1 percent of the fund's assets. The fund's top five holdings as a percentage of assets are currently: Genentech, Genzyme, Amgen, Pfizer, and Novartis.

At present, two-thirds of the portfolio is invested domestically, and a cash balance of around 5 percent is held for opportunities, including additional shares of existing companies and new investments, and redemptions. A recent example of a depressed investment, or a contrarian approach, involved the shares of Immunex in early 2001. The biotechnology company, which had developed treatments for arthritis and cancer, faced a setback during its trials with its new blockbuster drug Enbrel, used to treat rheumatoid arthritis. And later, the company ran into some production-capacity problems. Consequently, the stock fell precipitously. Believing in the company's efforts to overcome these hurdles, Sam bought shares at an average price of $13.55. At the end of 2001, the company agreed to be acquired for about $29.15 a share by biotechnology-giant Amgen. By this point, the position represented 4.5 percent of the fund.

Because many biotechnology companies are small and have early-stage or troubled product lines, they require a great deal of cash to stay alive. "We have generally avoided these pre-product companies," Sam says. "We prefer the biotech companies that are currently making money off existing product lines." Some of the top holdings currently in the fund that are U.S.-based include: Genentech (with 7.7 percent of assets); Amgen (6.1 percent); Genzyme (5.9 percent); and pharmaceutical-giant Pfizer (4.9 percent).

Sam is often asked why he invests outside the United States and subjects the portfolio to additional risks, such as currency fluctuation: "If all of the best biotechnology and pharmaceutical companies were located domestically, then we would be 100 percent invested domestically," he says. "The fact of the matter is, we've never seen a situation where all of the best opportunities for us have been in the United States. Although we currently have around 35 percent of the portfolio invested in foreign issues, that number has been as high as half when the right opportunities have arisen. We don't make any geographic allocations, we're just looking for return." On average, exposure is usually contained in two continents outside North America: 10 to 30 percent could be invested in Europe, and 10 to 20 percent in Asia. Currently, he is holding under 5 percent in cash. Unlike some funds that invest in foreign markets, Sam currently does not hedge the portfolio against adverse currency fluctuations.

"Our broad mission is to invest in the best opportunities anywhere in the world, considering risk and return," he continues. He attributes the fund's success to superior research and not overpaying for stocks. He seeks market-beating returns for investors, and to take less risk than his average peer.

Portfolio Composition

Breaking down the portfolio, around 20 percent of the fund's assets currently are invested in value picks, companies whose shares have fallen out of favor with investors. Some of these companies have included Abbott Labs and Immunex. Sam believes that companies such as these have great future potential, and the temporary prices of such declines are too tempting to pass up. For example, toward the end of 2001, Sam built a position in Genentech. Considered a value play, he felt the stock looked attractive when he bought it in the low 40s due to three new products it had in development, including Xaenelim, a medication for psoriasis, and treatments such as Avastin for solid-tumor cancers and Xolair for asthma. "The catalyst for this stock is the fact that each of these products could have a major impact," he says. And the firm's lymphoma drug Rituxan has continued to show strong sales.

Another 20 percent is allocated toward more speculative issues; each issue represents a small percentage of the fund, typically well under 1 percent of assets. An example of risk minimization includes an investment in Caliper Technologies, which was hurt by spending reductions in research and development among the big pharmaceutical companies. Sam's investment plummeted by 70 percent; fortunately, the position represented only a very small fraction of the portfolio, and was more than offset by a number of the fund's winning trades, including an investment in Immunex, which constituted 4.5 percent of the fund's assets at the time. In general, anywhere from 40 percent to 45 percent of the portfolio has been invested in biotechnology shares, compared to the Morningstar peer group's current average of 20 percent.

The remaining 60 percent have been generally allocated toward core holdings of pharmaceutical companies, such as Pfizer, Wyeth, Novartis, Lilly, and Sanofi. These issues—considered conservative among their peers—have tended to help smooth the fund's volatility that arose from the more speculative issues. Sam sums up the portfolio composition by saying, "We like to invest from the very earliest discovery all the way to the broadest distribution." When Sam speaks of discovery, he gives the example of a small biotechnology company that provides a product to a bigger company, or a company that offers enabling technology that can make a discovery process more efficient. Currently the portfolio is pretty evenly split between pharmaceutical and biotechnology stocks.

Sam generally avoids the service companies, such as HMOs and medical device companies, which include Guidant and Medtronic, because these companies have tended to underperform the biotechnology and pharmaceutical companies, and devices tend to have relatively short lives. "We think the largest potential returns are likely to be achieved in the therapeutics area in biotechnology and pharmaceuticals," he says. "There are some products in the device companies that could look attractive, and may see reasonable growth rates. In the services areas, we don't see potential rates of returns that are attractive to us."

Always straightforward and to the point, Sam simplifies some of the top elements that he seeks in a company: "Outstanding management, technological excellence, and strong potential for solid financial structure." He then points out that one of the most attractive elements of any company in which he invests, almost as important as a blockbuster vaccine, is management. "We are looking for management that is honest, intelligent, hardworking, and lucky," he says. He adds that the ideal company would possess the high level of integrity and work ethics that his team displays. "We have the same qualities that we are seeking in management," he says proudly.

Traditional and Nontraditional Measures

In general, Sam uses traditional and nontraditional value measures when selecting stocks. If the company is a large company, the traditional measures he considers include price-to–cash flow and market share growth potential. He adds that gross profit margins, which can be extremely high on a good patented product, is the reason he's more concerned about a product's acceptance in the marketplace, in terms of sales and market share, than current stated net profit. Nontraditional measures will include "value of market share" and "value of research resources."

For smaller companies, Sam first looks at the management. Next, he seeks novel technologies. The last piece he looks at is financial structure.

When evaluating the nontraditional technological measures, such as the potential of their technological programs, Sam will place heavier weightings on the nontraditional measures, and smaller weightings on other fundamentals; in fact, he will invest in a small company that holds great technological promise but is currently showing losses as long as he believes it is financially capable of waiting for its products, and revenue, to flourish. If the company lacks the financial strength to survive while waiting for its products to flourish, "it probably won't last, so there's no reason to get in." Companies that hold great promise but are not financially mighty are also candidates. "We believe that if the fundamentals are fixable, we might invest with the belief that a financially weak company could turn itself around." The fund's portfolio has tended to be balanced between young companies and established companies.

The relatively small number of holdings in the portfolio enables the analysts to focus and maintain close relations with management. He believes that a larger collection of holdings would result in less intensive examinations and open the door to surprises. "This intensive research and examinations behind each holding instills a great deal of conviction and confidence in our purpose," he says. "This also results in long holding periods."

The fund's average holding period is currently around four years, or a turnover ratio of about 25 percent. "Our investing horizon is long simply because we are seeking to buy good things and stay with them," he says. "If I could find a good company to hold forever, I would." When Sam has sold, 80 percent of the time it was due to a more attractive investment opportunity. The remaining 20 percent was due to a holding that was under-performing expectations.

One long-time holding, Geneva-based Serono S.A., has been part of the portfolio since 1989. The company is one of the three largest biotechnology companies, with revenues of around $2 billion for 2003. A world therapeutic leader in reproductive health, the biotechnology company also has had strong market positions in multiple sclerosis, growth, and metabolism. Additionally, the company is active in the research, development, production, and marketing of products that address several therapeutic areas.

When Sam was an independent analyst at a previous research company in the mid-eighties, he was already following the company for private equity investors. "They made chemicals for test tubes," he says in his simplistic and joking manner, referring to their fertility-enhancement business. "They make the drugs that enable women in their later and post-fertility years to get pregnant." In 1986, the company went public. When Sam began seeking investments for his newly developed fund in 1989, Serono was one of the first companies he put in his portfolio. He is still holding the stock, which is currently trading in the mid-20s, or around 30 times what he paid for it. His cost basis: around 80 cents. Because the Serono investment fell into the speculative portion of the investing spectrum, Sam limited his initial exposure to about 1 percent of total assets. "Since the introduction of its fertility drugs, the company's later products—such as strong market positions in neurology, metabolism, and growth—have maintained, and even increased, our exposure to the company." The company has since moved closer toward the conservative portion of the risk spectrum." Because Sam recognized the potential in the management and potential product line when he made his initial investment, he continued to hold the investment. Serono, now nearing its century mark, is currently the world's third-largest biotech firm.

Another former long-term holding, Biota, was part of the fund throughout most of the nineties. With a profit of around 30 times his initial investment, Sam found the company while researching the drug discovery business, and became fond of Biota's flu treatment. "Who wouldn't be intrigued by a company that could offer an end to the hacking, coughing, and sneezing to flu victims around the world?" During his research, he learned that the company formed an alliance with Glaxo. Pursuing his usual diligence, Sam contacted Glaxo to confirm. "Of course, this didn't attract much attention because at the time the hopes of a successful antiviral flu cure was still just a bunch of chemicals and a dream." Sam determined that the Biota team fit his criteria for high integrity, and saw the immense market potential. "During the critical advancement phase, the drug was already showing strong interest." Sam paid 35 cents a share for the company before it went public in 1986, and almost immediately it hit $1 as demand became far more intense. Prior to the introduction of the drug in the marketplace, the stock hit $8 a share. He sold the position between $8 and $10 a share in the late nineties.

Seeking Value

These more speculative ideas that Sam and team find are the result of intense research that Sam demands. "There's a four-year window that we consider the potential sweet spot of investing when it comes to discovery companies," he explains. "This represents the two years prior to the drug's introduction, and the two years after the launch. That's when you really see upside potential." He then adds: "Of course we'll hold them forever if it makes sense."

When it comes to determining the value of science and technology, "we don't pay any price, we want the right price—we want value," he says. "It works out nicely that about half of the team are scientists, while the other half are financial-oriented, including myself. This way, the financial people can keep the scientists grounded, and not believe that a drug that they are excited about is going to send the stock into the stratosphere. That's why we take a close look at the people, the science, and the financial situation. We can pretty much help only on the financial side, helping a company if it really makes sense to us."

Due to the nature of Sam's research process, focusing on management and scrutinizing the company's products, close contact and visitations are required. "We need to get to know the people running the show," Sam begins. "We determine whether they're honest, hard working, smart, and have common sense. I look for a history of successes, and we like them to be lucky." By luck, Sam is referring to the uncertainties and risks involved with new drugs, particularly when the drugs are in the trial runs with human beings. "We have almost always gotten the financials right, but we're subject to the risk of science." Sam points to Bayer's voluntary decision to discontinue the marketing and distribution of its cholesterol-lowering drug Baycol. "It was devastating to the company," he says. "It is related to over 100 deaths. This is one reason why we've built a team that can understand and even anticipate potential trouble."

When researching companies, Sam characterizes himself as an "Old Economy guy with a New Economy portfolio," referring to his clear understanding of fundamentals, such as cash flow, receivables, and inventories with a New Economy twist. This twist is his forward-looking ability in the technological areas, which represents the growth dynamics of the industry.

Going forward, Sam is optimistic about the industry's growth prospects. He believes the global pharmaceutical and biotechnology market—all companies, in all countries—could grow at a strong rate each year. He thinks biological science's technological advances are accelerating and will promote innovations, and that in five years we'll see a manyfold increase in the number of new products approved in the United States each year. In addition to high growth prospects, he expects the pharmaceutical, biotechnology, and health-care sectors to benefit from consolidation.

"Our fund hopes to continue to benefit from positive supply and demand," he says. He believes that the graying U.S. population, coupled with scientific breakthroughts in such areas as genomics and cancer treatment, sets the stage for an attractive trend. "If the past decade belonged to the technology investors, I think this next decade will belong to us." And as the economy rises, escalating incomes and economic statuses will lead people to spend a larger portion of their money on medicines. And while this industry isn't immune to tough economic times, health care profits generally don't decline during a recession. But the companies' growth does lessen. "During tough economic times, consumers tend to seek less expensive substitute drugs or procedures, which compresses profit margins." As an example, Sam mentions Merck's arthritis drug, Vioxx, which is more expensive than competing brands, but has fewer side effects. "Merck thought Vioxx would dominate this class of drugs, but its high price has led to a lower acceptance rate. Merck, as a result, issued a profit warning."

Sam points to Novartis as a company that offers a drug that is vastly superior to its peers. It is Gleevec, which treats chronic myeloid leukemia and that "works where nothing else does," he says. "Consequently, Novartis can command a premium price."

Sam adds, "This industry is like the field of dreams. As technology continues to rise at a rapid pace, new discoveries lead to cheaper alternatives or better treatments. It's one of those situations where if it's discovered, they will come."

Involvement with Portfolio Companies

Whether foreign or domestic, Sam's team physically meets with every company in the portfolio at least once a year. This is in addition to frequent conference calls and quarterly earnings reports. When meeting in person, the individual covering the company will meet with all levels of management. When necessary, Sam's team will make recommendations to the company regarding financial issues, or ideas to consider when planning product releases. When scrutinizing a company, Sam considers himself a "vicious interrogator." He says: "Sometimes they don't even know they are being interrogated, but I can usually learn something from any conversation."

Because the team becomes so knowledgeable and intimate with the companies in its portfolio, the team isn't shy about voicing opinions. Once, Sam's team led a proxy fight. The team opposed a $160 million acquisition of privately held Eos Biotechnology by biotechnology company Pharmacopeia. Health Sciences Fund owned 2.3 million shares of Pharmacopeia and secured support of another seven million shares, in all representing 10 percent of the outstanding common stock. "The deal was too expensive, especially at a time when we felt Pharmacopeia was undervalued. Additionally, the deal didn't make strategic sense and would have severely diluted Pharmacopeia earnings over the foreseeable future." Sam spoke to the firm's top management and pleaded his case. The CEO responded by saying they would proceed with the offer. Sam's team hired a proxy solicitation firm to help it garner additional shareholder support for its cause. Management at Pharmacopeia, believing that they were offering a fair price for Eos and that long-term benefits would be yielded for Pharmacopeia and its market value, responded by hiring consultants to help plead their case with investors. Sam's team won the proxy fight in February 2002. Always the gentleman and always seeking progress, Sam shook hands with Pharmacopeia's management and offered thoughts on how to build the company.

What does an all-star mutual fund manager, whose performance is extraordinary, consider a flop? Without hesitating, he utters, "Abgenix was my biggest failure." Why? "I ask myself why I didn't buy more. It rose so fast that I followed my discipline of selling it once it represented a high percentage of my portfolio."

CHAPTER FOURTEEN

BOB RODRIGUEZ

FPA
NEW
INCOME, INC.

› › ›

*B*ob Rodriguez's exceptional performance managing FPA New Income at First Pacific Advisors is nothing short of spectacular. Since he started managing the fund in 1984, his investors have never had a down year—a record unmatched by any other bond fund manager in the United States. His achievements haven't gone unnoticed: Bob was nominated for Fixed Income Manager of the Year in 2003 and won the 2001 Fixed Income Manager of the Year award by mutual fund tracking firm Morningstar, Inc. (He also won it in 1994; incredibly enough, this was also the second time he was nominated as an equity manager and a fixed income manager.) Bob simplifies his success to a handful of words: "Winning by not losing." Interestingly, this strategy he has carefully mastered over the years is the direct result of events that occurred before he was even born.

Early Lessons in Life

Living in Mexico, his father's family lost all their money in 1916, after the Revolution of 1910. The family faced many hardships. Five years later, his grandmother and six siblings immigrated from Mexico to California. There they found jobs and lived a better life. Although his father worked long hours, he found time late in the evenings to educate himself. Bob's father continued his self-education, and saved every penny to pursue his dream of going to college. After 12 years of saving, he was accepted to the University of Southern California. As he was preparing for college, he became very ill. All of his savings went to pay for his health recovery. His life was saved, but his dream was shattered.

This story affected Bob deeply when he was a child and would resonate in his mind for the rest of his life. Even though his father's discipline to educate himself rewarded him with a modest-paying position as a chemical engineer, the family had to be very careful with money. Bob was well aware of how diligently his parents saved over the years, meticulously planning for their future: college, retirement, and, of course, any unknowns that might occur.

Perhaps that's why, growing up, Bob was always interested in money. Even in his early elementary school years he was not only trading coins, but also committing large volumes of currency data to memory—types of coins, grades, and values. In the fifth grade, as an English assignment his teacher asked the students to write a letter to someone other than a friend or family member, and receive something back. While other students were writing to the local barber, candy storeowner, and high-school football coach, Bob consulted the librarian for advice. Knowing the student's interest in the dynamics of money—one of his favorite games was banker and borrower—she showed him a book called *A History of the Federal Reserve of the United States* (Vol. 1, 1913–1915, Chicago: University of Chicago Press). He opened the book to the beginning and saw an introduction written by William McChesney Martin, then-Chairman of the Federal Reserve.

The young Rodriguez wrote a letter to the Chairman, describing the class exercise and requesting general information about the workings of the Federal Reserve. A few weeks later, a large brown envelope arrived at the Rodriguez residence addressed to Bob. Inside was a letter from the Chairman thanking Bob for his interest and offering him a subscription to the *Federal Reserve Bulletin*. In addition, the Chairman wrote that Bob was the youngest subscriber in the history of the Federal

Reserve. Shortly thereafter, Bob developed a keen interest in the New York Stock Exchange and determined that he would go to college and study business.

Bob wanted to attend a local state university because it was less expensive than a private university such as the University of Southern California. He wanted to study business and thought that USC would be the best, but "I didn't want to go there because I knew my father couldn't afford a private school," Bob recollects. "But, thinking back on his own life, my father insisted and said he would do whatever it took to pay for it." Bob contributed to his college bills by taking out loans and working a full-time job. He graduated in 1971 magna cum laude with a bachelor's degree in business. At the time he was offered a fellowship for graduate work at USC, but declined because he wanted to get some investing experience under his belt. Three years later, after working as a securities trader and financial analyst at an insurance company, he returned to USC for his graduate degree and fellowship. Unfortunately, "private university endowments were destroyed in the down markets, particularly in 1974," he says, "with some portfolios down 40 to 60 percent. It was devastating." Additionally, in 1972 Bob invested his savings in a stock when it was trading in the low 20s. He averaged down with the remainder of his savings, buying more shares as the stock dropped to $8 a share. The stock dropped to under $1 a share. "Once again," says Bob, "I learned another lesson about losing money."

Bob managed to work his way through graduate school, all the while diligently studying the mechanics of the stock market. "At the time, several companies were selling at less than the value of cash on their balance sheet, net of all debt," he explains, "including the stock that I owned. To see capital destroyed and how difficult it is to recover left an indelible mark on my mind."

He was also perplexed: "I didn't understand how one could buy cash at a discount," he says. "That's when I discovered the classic book *Security Analysis*, written by Benjamin Graham and David Dodd." The student was fascinated by the carefully honed methods for finding undervalued stocks and bonds.

Building a Career

After graduating with his MBA in 1975, Bob continued to work for the insurance company, then joined another insurance company with an associate of his. Their job was to turn around the investment portfolio. "At the time, portfolios weren't marked to market," he says, referring to the now-required accounting procedure whereby portfolios are valued at the current market value rather than at historical cost. This company's portfolio was down around 40 percent, which was common for insurance portfolios. In other words, they were basically insolvent," he says, shaking his head with a smile. "They gave us the mission of getting the fund back to parity—without interest rates dropping by eight percentage points!" he adds sarcastically.

"We gradually shifted the portfolio to a much heavier equity weighting. We utilized gains from the equities to offset losses from bonds. With this strategy, we were able to bring the portfolio back to parity. We were able to take advantage of the valuation dislocations that were caused by bond yields in the 20 percent range." Bob's strategy would later become useful in managing both stocks and bonds.

With the remainder of the industry still mired in losses of 20 percent or more, they were considered very successful. Yet Bob still wanted to pursue his own ambition: to manage his own mutual fund. He left the insurance company in 1983 and joined First Pacific Advisors (FPA).

When Bob approached First Pacific Advisors to manage investment portfolios, they were in the process of acquiring what would be later named FPA New Income and FPA Capital Fund. The principals asked him what his goals were. Without flinching, he said: "Professionally, to make investors money. Personally, to simultaneously be one of the top bond managers and equity managers." (He was once simultaneously in the top 10 on the equity side and number 11 on the bond side for a 10-year period.)

With his previous experience at the insurance company, managing both equities and bonds seemed very natural to him.

He was given the job of managing both FPA Capital Fund, with $38 million in assets, and FPA New Income, with $4.5 million. (The funds now each have over $1 billion in assets.) In the case of FPA Capital, Bob learned a valuable lesson as he once again turned around a fund that was steeped in losses. "I learned that people don't forget," he says. "Investors were devastated in this fund along with the disastrous equity markets in the first half of the seventies. It occurred to me that every time the fund neared ten dollars a share, we received a raft of redemptions." He learned that these were the investors who originally bought the fund's shares at its initial offering price of $10: "Back in 1967!" he exclaims. "They just wanted to get even and get out. As a professional investor who seeks trends, I feel it's important to realize that people have very long memories." During his first three years managing FPA Capital he witnessed $10 million in redemptions leave the fund.

Shareholders First

For the bond-oriented FPA New Income, Bob immediately restructured the way it would invest its capital. Rather than following the other bond funds at the time and becoming sector focused or buying high-quality bonds and holding to maturity (high-yield/junk bonds were not yet considered a category), he insisted on being different. "Sector funds experience too much extreme volatility, particularly if you're in a sector that remains out of favor for a prolonged period of time," he says. "This, I believed, was not the smartest strategy for a bond or equity portfolio."

Once Bob started showing positive results, he traveled nationwide pitching his strategies to mutual fund investors and pension investors. Bob's genuine sense of caring for his investors' money has been so discernible that today he is proud to have retained even his earliest investors—both institutional and retail investors.

One way in which he has cared about his investors is shown in his expense ratio, or the fee that mutual fund companies levy on investors that comes directly out of performance. "I am proud of the fact that New Income has had declining costs over that entire period of time and as of today its expense ratio is at 61 basis points," he says gratifyingly. "We think about the shareholder first. We may not be great marketers, or even make as much money as other fund managers, but our investors sure are benefiting from a higher total return, after expenses." In reality, investors probably wouldn't even mind higher fees, considering Bob's superior performance.

A Contrarian Approach

Bob's initial strategy evolved around the relationship between bonds and inflation. "Essentially, when bonds were trading at wide real yield spreads, a premium of 500 basis points, or five percentage points, above the consumer price index, we would deem bonds attractive. We would invest in longer-duration bonds," he says, referring to bonds whose average payments of interest and principal are paid out over a very long period of time. "When the inflation spread widens, there is general uncertainty about either the economic environment or the financial environment, or fear of some type of crisis." This is when the average bond investor is selling, and Bob is generally buying. When the spread narrows, Bob starts selling at a profit and begins to shorten the fund's average duration. "When inflation spreads and quality spreads are narrowing, it's just the opposite; investors are feeling better about the climate for investing, so they are buying again." This is when Bob prefers to sell. The bonds he focused his investment toward were typically investment-grade securities, mortgage-backed securities (bonds that are backed by the underlying collateral of real-estate loans), high-yield corporate bonds, or convertible securities. Convertible bonds pay less interest than traditional corporate bonds, but can be exchanged for a specified number of common shares at a predetermined conversion price; these securities rise in price as the underlying stock is rising, but when stocks fall, the prospect of conversion dims, and the bond drops in price.

When Bob would make a bet on yield spreads, or the difference in yield between a bond and a similar-maturity Treasury bond, he would focus on mortgage bonds and corporate bonds. "When the economy is picking up, investors start factoring in inflation risk, which tends to lead to higher interest rates," he explains. "This is when Treasuries start dropping in price, bringing their yields higher. Additionally, high-credit quality bonds will drop because their cost of financing is increasing. Conversely, distressed securities [the term high-yield securities wasn't widely used until several years later] and busted convertible bonds [convertible securities that typically trade below 70 percent of par or $1,000, resulting in the conversion feature having a limited value; the bond will thus trade like a conventional bond] will be appreciating because the economy is improving and business prospects are looking up. We focus on high-quality and high-yield and mix them together into a portfolio that has a credit barbell emphasis. This strategy can enhance the overall return of the portfolio while dampening the overall portfolio volatility. In essence, you have two different security structures that effectively have a low correlation coefficient, or the degree to which two variables move together. High-yield securities have different volatility curves from those of higher-quality bonds."

This strategy enables Bob to keep money working at all times, while minimizing risk. "Most bond managers stick to high-quality bonds or high-yield bonds," he says. "If that were me, I'd have high cash levels part of the time until I felt we were being compensated sufficiently, through a higher yield, to take on credit or maturity risk. Many money managers, however, are required to be nearly fully invested at all times and have a portfolio duration that is not far from their benchmark index. This is unreasonable to me since rarely is a sector attractively valued all the time in its area of specialty."

Bob explains, "The least amount of busted convertibles/high-yield securities we've held has been 2 percent out of our maximum allowable of 25 percent. If we were a sector bond manager, we'd in effect be only 8 percent invested and 92 percent in cash. How many sector-fund managers would be able to go to that extreme? Pretty much none. Our overriding strategy, in effect, is to be contrarians. We buy securities when they hate them; sell them when they love them. Or, when fear is in the marketplace and bond managers are defensive in terms of shorter durations and high-quality bonds, we will be invested in busted convertibles or high-yield securities and longer-duration high-quality bonds."

He offers an example dating back to 1984. "Interest rates were rapidly climbing, partly due to the Continental Illinois Bank crisis. We bought 14 percent zero coupon bonds." Because zero coupon Treasury bonds pay all accrued interest and principal at maturity, they are considered to have the longest duration. "Nobody wanted them," he says. "In April 1987, the 30-year Treasury bond traded at a yield of about 7 percent, down from the 14 percent level in 1984," he remembers. "This was a 700-basis- point yield rally in about three years." The zero coupon bonds soared in price. "Interest rates at this point were relatively low because people were optimistic about inflation and the economy; consequently, investors were bullish on bonds."

With all the bullishness, Bob knew it was time to become bearish on interest rates. Betting on an increase in interest rates, he looked at the newly formed collateralized mortgage-backed bond obligation (CMO) market. These bonds are backed by pools of residential mortgages. Two types of CMOs are interest-only (IO) securities and principal-only (PO) securities. Because homeowners tend to refinance their mortgages when interest rates drop, IO securities will drop in price rapidly as the underlying mortgages are prepaid and no more interest will come due. POs, on the other hand, will rally in price because the principal is returned sooner; these derivative securities tend to be very volatile. In this case, Bob was betting that interest rates would rise, so he bought IO securities, which would benefit from a dearth of prepayments and more time to collect interest, thus raising the price of the securities.

The IOs he bought were part of the first mortgage-backed derivative ever to be issued, called Fannie Mae Trust 1. Because investors were so bullish on interest rates, IOs were trading at cheap levels. Later, when interest rates rose, the value of Bob's IOs likewise rose.

The Top-Down Approach

Because of his unique contrarian approaches, Bob is considered both a bottom-up investor, seeking specific issues that are out-of-favor and undervalued, and a top-down investor, considering macro events such as politics and the economy, then looking at sectors, then specific securities. When using the top-down approach, he feels you can't ignore macroeconomic issues "because in the bond market everything essentially rises and falls together. I avoid making major decisions as to the direction of macroeconomic issues, such as changing my viewpoint on interest rates from bearish to bullish overnight. I just don't think anybody can reliably make those calls. Since I realize I'm no smarter than anybody else at making timing calls, I essentially diversify my decisions in terms of time frames. Over time, I will make multiple sales or purchases. I will also further diversify by purchasing or selling at different price levels. By diversifying my decisions, I can minimize the risk of any one decision."

When modeling potential outcomes of macroeconomic events, "we rely on probabilities," Bob explains. "Because nobody can consistently and accurately forecast interest rates, we just look at the odds of what's occurring." He offers 1993 as an example. "The yield curve was at an extremely steep level between the three-month Treasury bill and the 30-year Treasury bond. This was due to the Fed's aggressive lowering of interest rates. Many investors were reaching for yield; that is, investing in longer maturities for the higher yield levels. I stayed with the short-term rates of 3 percent, willing to give up the extra two percentage points of income. By October 1993, at about the time short-term interest rates hit their lows, we figured that bond investors weren't being compensated for maturity or credit risk, and, therefore, there was virtually no value in the bond market. To us, this was a clear sign of overvaluation. At that point, we positioned our portfolio so the duration was very short, thus minimizing the risk of principal loss if interest rates should happen to increase. Lo and behold, in 1994, the bond market experienced its worst market in the last 100 years with a dramatic rise in rates when the Federal Reserve tightened credit. We were pleased to have protected our investors' assets during that period of time." (From February 4, 1994 to December 31, 1994, FPA New Income was up 0.71 percent, while the 10-year Treasury was down 7.48 percent and the Lehman/Brothers Government/Credit was down 4.39 percent.)

Bob positioned the portfolio so that the overall duration was two years, a very conservative posture. "We were in high-quality mortgage-backed bonds, short-duration Treasury securities, and cash," he adds. "We had a very low exposure to high-yield securities, which we felt were risky because we felt business conditions would deteriorate. On the other hand, those investors who sought the longer-maturity bonds for the higher current yields destroyed significant amounts of capital."

At the beginning of 1994, one pension client fired him, telling Bob he was erring in judgment. "I basically stayed out of the markets for about two years because I simply couldn't find enough value," Bob explains. "I couldn't convince them that better opportunities would exist down the road." Indeed, in February the Federal Reserve began raising interest rates, "and the worst bond market in 100 years ensued, and the equity markets also went down. I was disappointed that this particular client's time frame was too shortsighted."

Minimizing Risk

Bob is clear to point out that FPA does not make any forecasts. "We will never say interest rates are going to X percent by a certain date," he says. "We'll tend to say, 'Given an increase in rates, how much could we lose?' We look at it from the standpoint of probabilities of what could we lose in a year if we are wrong." As an example, "when the ten-year Treasury rose from 4.18 percent to 5.2 percent in the extremely short period between November and December 2001, it produced a negative 6.84 percent return. That was the worst high-quality bond return period in the history of the bond market." During that time period, FPA New Income achieved a positive return of 79 basis points, or 0.79 percent. "We looked at that ten-year 4 percent yield as being dangerous," he says. "It doesn't take much of a move to wipe out one year's worth of income. It seemed more like a defla-tionary bet than anything else. For the year, FPA New Income returned 12.3 percent, nearly 5 percentage points ahead of the average mutual fund in the intermediate-term bond category, and almost 4 percentage points ahead of the fund's index, the Lehman Brothers Aggregate Index.

"Generally the higher the yield, the greater the margin of safety," he says. "I find it interesting that when yields were double digit, as they were in the early eighties, individual and professional investors wanted to main-tain short durations because they were fearful of what might happen. Then when rates were low, and confidence high, what did individuals and pro-fessionals do? They ran out and bought longer-duration bonds. It's the same thing every single cycle. It amazes me."

While many bond managers are required to be entirely invested in bonds, Bob prefers his point of view. "Our clients are paying us to exercise our best judgment. Sometimes they may agree with us and sometimes they may not." Indeed, his track record speaks for itself.

In general, Bob seeks a total return in excess of inflation, that is, a real return on capital. His ideal target is 400 basis points over the implied infla-tion rate. As far as portfolio composition, he is mandated to invest at least 75 percent of the fund's assets in bonds rated double-A or better. "On av-erage, 65 to 75 percent of the assets have been invested in securities of government agencies." Up to 25 percent of the fund can be invested in se-curities rated below double-A.

"When buying corporate bonds, particularly those high-yield securi-ties, or busted convertible bonds," Bob says, "I like to bring an element of expertise and insight into the companies which we're looking at. Most of the time, the corporate bonds we're buying are under price pressure, so we like to understand what's going on." When looking at bonds, he per-forms the same type of research on a company that he would do for a stock that he is buying for his FPA Capital Fund. "I look at factors such as whether a company has a strong competitive position in their market-place, cash flow, and nature of the business. We tear apart both the balance sheet and the income statement. We want to know what are the key drivers of the business."

For example, one holding is Oregon Steel Mills bonds. The issue, comprising 0.67 percent of the fund, is paying 10 percent interest and has a six-year maturity. "There are two reasons we like these bonds. First, these are first-mortgage bonds that are backed by the most modern part of their steel mills. We consider the value of the assets to be greater than the bond's value. Second, their business is considerably different from that of other steel companies. They focus on specialty grades of steel that go into natural-gas pipeline-construction projects for a large portion of their business. They are one of only a few companies in the United States that provide this product. They are also one of only two U.S. companies that produce rail track—the other is Bethlehem Steel. Currently, the company is fully backlogged for its pipeline-steel capacity. These bonds are likely to be refinanced before their maturity."

He is permitted to buy up to 15 percent of the portfolio in derivative securities, although they usually comprise at most 10 percent. The derivatives he will buy tend to be CMOs. Corporate bonds and derivative securities represent Bob's bottom-up approach to security selection.

The Bottom-Up Approach

Bob's bottom-up approach tends to be more opportunistic trading. For example, when Treasury Inflation Protected Securities (TIPS), were first issued in 1997, Bob initially opposed investing in the securities. At the time, he was on a panel with other leading money managers discussing the new securities. He told them, "I wouldn't buy them." The panelists looked at him in surprise, as the securities gained widespread approval in the investment community as a worthy hedge against inflation for fixed-income investors. (TIPS are similar to conventional Treasury bonds except that principal and coupon payments are adjusted according to the latest consumer price index figures to eliminate the effects of inflation.

Consequently, the bonds offer a "real" rate of return instead of one that is nominal.)

Bob told the panelists that he did not trust the federal government because "I'm afraid that they may change the composition of the index, and I don't think the spreads on the TIPS are high enough to compensate me for what I would call governmental index risk." Sure enough, soon after the first TIPS were issued, the federal government reformulated the way the CPI was calculated. "Once they adjusted the CPI, the yield went up, and higher effective yields were offered on the TIPS."

To put it in perspective, Bob says, when the TIPS were first issued they yielded around 3.27 percent, plus an additional increment, which is the implied inflation rate. Bob bought the bonds between yields of 3.7 percent all the way up to 4.3 percent—"over 100 basis points higher than where they were issued." His average weight-adjusted yield is now just over 4 percent. Bob's assistant portfolio manager, Tom Atteberry, analyzed the difference between buying the TIPS versus purchasing a nominal 10-year Treasury bond. "We've earned a higher annual total rate of return—in excess of 100 basis points—with 67 percent less volatility." Even with relatively generic securities, such as Treasuries, Bob is able to use a bottom-up approach to find value.

Another time, in 1985, investors feared that the Tennessee Valley Authority would lose its status as a governmental agency. Consequently, the agency's bond spreads widened by over 100 basis points. Bob determined that this scenario would be highly unlikely. As investors' fears diminished over the coming months, the spread quickly narrowed by 80 basis points, enabling Bob to sell his large position at a profit.

The vast array of security types that Bob will pursue requires extensive research, which is all performed in-house. On the fixed-income side, Bob relies mostly on Tom in high-quality bonds, but also counts on the expertise of Steven Romick, portfolio manager of FPA Crescent Fund, and Steven Geist, co-manager of FPA Perennial Fund and fixed income manager for Source Capital, Inc.

When seeking opportunistic investments, the team is on the constant

hunt for areas of the markets that are "getting destroyed or where pessimism resides," he says. "We are constantly looking for anything that Wall
Street is throwing away or fearful of, because that increases the odds that a
security or sector is mispriced."

Winning by Not Losing

Bob's style of preserving principal is evident in the way he buys most of
the fund's securities. "When we're buying a security we're always asking
ourselves, 'If we're wrong, can we live with it?' If we can answer 'yes,' then
we'll own the security. Often our assumption when buying is so conservative that we automatically assume that we're going to have to sit with the
security for a long period of time. Our focus on avoiding losing money has
resulted in FPA New Income generally outperforming the bond market in
stable to rising interest-rate environments. This is what I mean when I say
'we win by not losing.'" This long-term line of thinking also benefits his
investors tax-wise: Ever since he's been managing the fund, the turnover
rate has been less than 52 percent, meaning the average holding period for
an investment is about three years. His peers' average is about 100 percent.

When asked how he measures risk, Bob declares that there is no good
way to do it. "We're always looking at the duration, but we really keep an
eye on the risk of losing money," he says. "Since we have pretty conservative investors, seeking a safe place for their money but interested in a nice
return, we try to accomplish both those objectives.

"Most measure risk as volatility, or the standard deviation of returns,"
he says skeptically. "But that doesn't really measure risk; it just measures
volatility. In my career, I have not seen a valid definition of risk or how
to measure it. I'm a believer in such risks as interest-rate risk, credit-
quality risk, currency risk, liquidity risk, and so on. Volatility is just one
aspect of risk, so we attempt to moderate it because the only way to
eliminate it is to invest in money-market instruments, but then you're up
against substandard returns over a 10-, 20- or 30-year time period. With
FPA New Income, we're all about high returns and very low volatility. In

fact, our volatility is somewhere around 35 percent of the average bond fund, yet our returns are higher than our benchmark index and the average bond fund.

"Our unique approach of pursuing a credit barbell—high-quality and low-quality bonds—while subduing volatility, has successfully resulted in the best relative returns. We're constantly amazed that more managers haven't pursued this seemingly simple style of management."

For individual investors, Bob believes FPA New Income is well suited for those with a conservative total-return outlook, willing to take on some risk. For investors concerned about taxes, the fund should be kept in a nontaxable account, such as a retirement account. He feels that anyone under 85 years of age or so should be seeking a bond fund that focuses on total return, that is, capital appreciation plus income, and not current yield. Funds and investors who focus mostly on current yield will almost always be purchasing the most overvalued sectors of the bond market.

How does an all-star manager of FPA New Income, the equity-oriented FPA Capital Fund, and separate accounts—all worth nearly $4 billion—spend each day? Surely he must find time to talk to investors, follow dozens of market sectors, and gauge the outcome of myriad investing scenarios. He jokes: "It's a lot easier than in the eighties when I was a one-man team juggling everything."

The day begins at five in the morning at his home outside Los Angeles taking calls from the East Coast, and reading to keep abreast of market events. He walks into the office by 8:30 A.M., when all financial markets are open. It helps that he has a long-term outlook for his investments, for this enables him to focus on research reports, communicate with companies in which he invests or contemplates an investment, and compare and contrast different investments against one another looking for value. He leaves the office by seven in the evening; at home he spends a few hours reading additional research and other related materials. By 11:30 P.M., he "hits the sack hard." Bob balances his hard work, and perhaps his aversion to risk, with hard play as an amateur racecar driver. He races Porsches. In this sport, you really have to balance reward versus risk.

Hard Work and Heavy Responsibility

He feels that all the hard work and heavy responsibility involved in implementing his strict investing philosophy are more than worth the result—his outstanding success as a fund manager. "My entire team at FPA takes such great pride in our work," he says. "We have a high level of ethics, integrity, and discipline, and I think that's why we're successful. And we're very thrilled that we can help so many individuals pursue their dreams. This is what it's all about."

INDEX